Praise for
What Happy Working Mothers Know

"*What Happy Working Mothers Know* highlights the diversity, strength, and creativity these women bring to the workplace. They can become role models for others, and their knowledge and skills add value and can help everyone bring their best to work every day."
—Joel A. Stern, Deputy General Counsel, Accenture

"With this important book, Cathy Greenberg and Barrett Avigdor expand the strengths movement to parenting as well as work. They show that working to your strengths not only maximizes your contribution at work but it makes you a better parent as well. As a father and a leader in the strengths movement, this book energizes and inspires me."
—Marcus Buckingham, author of *Find Your Strongest Life: What the Happiest and Most Successful Women Do Differently*

"As a working mother myself, it's encouraging to see such a wonderful book that is relatable to all women. Delightful, inspiring, and motivating. This book really hit home for me."
—Kim Martin, President and General Manager, WE tv

"In *What Happy Working Mothers Know*, Cathy Greenberg continues to demonstrate an outstanding intellect with impeccable credentials and experience as both an executive and a working mother. This insightful and creative book with Barrett Avigdor will contribute to a rich human harvest for both working mothers and their organizations. *What Happy Working Mothers Know* is an innovative resource for leadership."
—Warren Bennis, Distinguished Professor of Business Administration at the Marshall School of Business, University of Southern California; founding Chairman of Marshall School's Leadership Institute

"Women everywhere will recognize themselves in this book. No matter where they are on the career ladder, working mothers can move beyond mere success and achieve true satisfaction: A happy, balanced life that sets a positive tone for those around them. Sounds impossible? Cathy Greenberg and Barrett Avigdor show us how in this splendid work, chock full of wisdom, anecdotes, and real-life action steps and advice."
—Carolyn Kepcher, CEO Carolyn & Co; co-star of NBC's *The Apprentice*

"Greenberg and Avigdor provide a mix of fact-based research, practical tools, and a large dose of high-energy inspiration to help you reach for both your happiness and your best performance every day. A groundbreaking book that will become a mainstay for working moms, those who may become working moms, and for everyone who both manages and loves working moms."
—Sara N. King, Center for Creative Leadership

"Mothers occupy one of the top two spots on the short list of leader role models—way ahead of political leaders, business leaders, community leaders, and military leaders. That's why it's so vitally important that working mothers focus not just on their career success, but also on their happiness. Their moods are contagious—at home and at work—and when moms can radiate great joy wherever they are, it will go a long way to developing positive and productive people. In *What Happy Working Mothers Know*, Cathy Greenberg and Barrett Avigdor shine a bright light on the leadership challenges of working mothers, offering practical tools and revealing case studies that will enable mothers to get extraordinary things done; and also to grow the future leaders we so desperately need."
—Jim Kouzes, award-winning coauthor of the bestseller, *The Leadership Challenge*; and Dean's Executive Professor of Leadership, Leavey School of Business, Santa Clara University

"Good leaders tap into the best in each of us. They inspire and motivate. They help us see possibilities where others see problems. This book, *What Happy Working Mothers Know*, shows that happiness is an essential element of good leadership—both at work and at home."
—Dee Dee Myers, author of *Why Women Should Rule the World*; and former press secretary for President Bill Clinton (the first woman in that job)

"It's great to see a book that celebrates the working mother and its benefits for the family. It truly fits into our family credo: 'It's all how you look at it.'"
—Dan Patrick, host of *The Dan Patrick Show*; co-host of NBC's *Football Night in America*; and senior writer for *Sports Illustrated*; and Susan Patrick, mother of four, gourmet ice cream entrepreneur/owner of Walnut Beach Creamery

"Philips is very proud to have been an early supporter and part of the research for this book. As a global leader in our industries, we understand the power of a diverse workforce but it is not always easy to harness that power. The research that Greenberg and Avigdor have done has given us insights into new ways to tap into the incredible energy and strength of working mothers in our workforce."
—Anne LeGrand, CEO Ultrasound, Philips Healthcare

"I have the privilege of working with hundreds of women year after year and I am thrilled to see *What Happy Working Mothers Know* touch on such an important topic. Women tend to focus on the 'what' they are (mother, daughter, sister, leader, co-worker, friend) but not always the 'how' (happy, fulfilled, joyous, passionate) Adding the concept of happiness and contentment to the equation of being a working woman is a life changer. To focus on creating contentment, abundance, and richness of spirit in the work of motherhood is not what women instinctively learn. Women are taught to sacrifice, put themselves last, and to do for everyone else. This book reminds all of us to make the happiness decision, to choose the 'how' our life will look and feel. Bravo!"
—Grace Killelea, VP of Talent and Leadership Initiatives, Comcast

"*What Happy Working Mothers Know* is filled with touching stories, clarity, and insight, which can only help build on the strengths of our Hispanic community and continue to grow our women leaders, as well as the wonderful leaders that they will raise for a brighter tomorrow."
—Rev. Luis Cortés Jr., founder and president of Esperanza, the largest Hispanic faith-based evangelical network in the country

"One of the most important books for working mothers in the new world!"
—Marshall Goldsmith, best-selling coauthor of *What Got You Here Won't Get You There* and author of *Succession: Are You Ready?*

"This is a very important book in these turbulent times as our future is dependent on how we nurture and develop society's most valued human asset, the next generation. Cathy Greenberg and Barrett Avigdor provide an extraordinarily helpful and inspiring guide to the many woman and men who care about our future."
—Noel Tichy, professor, University of Michigan; and author of *Judgment: How Winning Leaders Make Great Calls*

"*What Happy Working Mothers Know* combines the science of happiness with new findings in positive psychology to help both working mothers and the people who love them, and works with them to be their best. Greenberg and Avigdor apply data and real-world stories to celebrate the relationship between whole-brain function and decision-making for higher performance at home and on the job."
—Shawn Anchor, Harvard University researcher; Harvard head teaching fellow; and CEO of Aspirant Consulting

"*What Happy Working Mothers Know* is a powerfully positive and uplifting book that can help you immediately bring more happiness into your life and the lives of others. Practical and filled with great wisdom, I highly recommend this book."
—Daniel G. Amen, M.D., author of *Magnificent Mind at Any Age*

"As part of our commitment to creating compelling careers for women in Philips Corporation, we participated actively in the research for this book. Our investment has paid off in a book that gives practical guidance, both to employers and to individual women, as to how to maximize their productivity and success at home and at work."
—Britt van den Berg, Director, Global Diversity and Inclusion, Philips International

"*What Happy Working Mothers Know*, above all else, is that happiness drives success, more than the other way around. Use the wisdom of this book to inspire you to create your happiness as a working mother, which of course is a redundant term!"
—Steve Bonner, CEO, Cancer Treatment Centers of America

"*What Happy Working Mothers Know* brings an exciting new concept of the contribution that leaders who are women and are mothers make to the enterprise, the organization. Leaders in all three sectors, men and women, will welcome this wisdom that benefits us all."
—Frances Hesselbein, Chairman and founding President, Leader to Leader Institute, New York

"Greenberg and Avigdor show that being a mom is great leadership training and can make you better at your job, no matter what job you do."
—Mark Goulston, M.D., author of *Get Out of Your Own Way at Work . . . and Help Others Do the Same*

"There are lots of books out there about how to survive as a working woman. This book goes beyond it to show how working women can actually thrive. Greenberg and Avigdor never forget what women really want: to find and spread happiness and joy."
—Sally Helgesen, author of *Thriving in 24/7: The Female Advantage*

"*What Happy Working Mothers Know* demonstrates how one act of kindness towards yourself to create the most powerful positive story about you can truly transform your life both at work and at home."
—Jim Loehr, co-founder of the Human Performance Institute, and author of *The Power of Story: Change Your Story, Change Your Destiny in Business and in Life*

"Greenberg and Avigdor share insights to help any company understand how to improve life satisfaction and work satisfaction to increase happy leaders in the ranks. Supporting evolving women leaders maximizes returns on people as well as return on profit."
—Bill Lombardo, Senior Director, Bankers Learning Network, Bankers Life and Casualty Company

"Greenberg and Avigdor are the coaches we all wish we had—smart, helpful, and supportive. This book is like getting a few coaching sessions from the best coaches out there. Even better, it teaches you to coach yourself through the challenges and joys of being a working mom."
—Linda R. Manfredonia, J.D., L.L.M., Chief Fiduciary Officer/Regional Managing Director, PNC Wealth Management

"While I speak about educating women to fuel the economic growth of a country and building global capabilities, this book explains how working mothers nurture themselves and, at the same time, develop our future global leaders. You will be happier just reading this book!"
—Blythe McGarvie, best-selling author of *Shaking the Globe: Courageous Decision-Making in a Changing World*

"Working moms have finally gotten the help they need. They no longer have to cut corners with their families to be successful on the job, or put their careers on hold while they raise their kids. They can excel at home and at work—and choose to find fulfillment for themselves on their own terms. With the science of positive psychology as their starting point, Greenberg and Avigdor draw on the stories of women who show how it is done. This is an essential how-to book for any working mom committed to taking of herself even as she takes care of everybody else."
—Mario Moussa, coauthor of *The Art of Woo: Using Strategic Persuasion to Sell Your Ideas;* and Principal, Center for Applied Research Inc.

"Happiness isn't a 'nice to have as a mother or an executive'; if you want your kids to have the most healthy brains possible—it's an essential quality to develop. Happy parents equals happy workers equals happy kids equals healthy, long, and productive lives. Well done to Cathy and Barrett for a writing a great book that can help with all of this."
—David Rock, founder, The NeuroLeadership Institute and Results Coaching
     Systems; and author of *Your Brain at Work*

"Many of our members are working mothers at various stages of their professional journey, experiencing the many stresses and strains, pushes and pulls of their careers and personal lives. Our role at WICT is to provide resources to help them along their professional journey, and this book will provide them with a rich tool filled with fact-based research, practical tips, and inspiration to help them reach for their happiness every day."
—Laurie Root, Vice President, Education and Program Development, Women in
     Cable Telecommunications

"Greenberg and Avigdor provide readers with realistic tools and a hefty dose of inspiration to help in their pursuit of happiness. As someone who is a working woman but not a mom, it has brought me closer to understanding and appreciating those working moms I love."
—Elaina S. Spilove, CIMA, President, Association of Professional Investment
     Consultants

"Lost in the debate over working vs. stay-at-home motherhood is the fact that kids are not happy if mom is not happy, fulfilled, and in control of her family's financial security. Contrary to societal stereotypes and distorted news headlines, many of the 80 million moms in America know firsthand that working motherhood equals happy motherhood. Here are the secrets straight from moms who are living the happy life."
—Leslie Morgan Steiner, editor of *Mommy Wars: Stay-at-Home and Career Moms
     Face Off on Their Choices, Their Lives, Their Families*; and columnist for *Mommy
     Track'd: Managing the Chaos of Modern Motherhood*

"This terrific guidebook is for every mother who has felt burned out, stretched in 12 directions, and ready to go back to bed by 10:00 a.m. Packed with practical exercises based on scientific research, *What Happy Working Mothers Know* is the perfect antidote to the joy-crushing, rat-race mentality. There's no quick fix to the crushing responsibility of juggling work and motherhood, but this book clearly shows that happiness is within your grasp."
—Jamie Woolf, author of *Mom-in-Chief: How Wisdom from the Workplace
     Can Save Your Family from Chaos*

What
Happy
Working Mothers
Know

What
Happy
Working Mothers
Know

How New Findings in Positive
Psychology Can Lead to a Healthy
and Happy Work/Life Balance

CATHY L. GREENBERG, Ph.D
AND
BARRETT S. AVIGDOR, J.D.

WILEY

John Wiley & Sons, Inc.

Published by John Wiley & Sons, Inc., Hoboken, New Jersey.
Published simultaneously in Canada.

For general information on our other products and services or for technical support, please contact our Customer Care Department within the United States at (800) 762–2974, outside the United States at (317) 572–3993 or fax (317) 572–4002.

Wiley also publishes its books in a variety of electronic formats. Some content that appears in print may not be available in electronic books. For more information about Wiley products, visit our web site at www.wiley.com.

Library of Congress Cataloging-in-Publication Data:

Greenberg, Cathy.

What happy working mothers know : how new findings in positive psychology can lead to a healthy and happy work/life balance / by Cathy L. Greenberg and Barrett S. Avigdor.
    p. cm.
Includes bibliographical references and index.
ISBN 978-0-470-48819-5 (cloth)
  1. Working mothers–Psychology.   2. Working mothers–Attitudes.
  3. Work and family.   4. Happiness. I. Avigdor, Barrett S. II. Title.
HQ759.48.G74 2010
155.6'463–dc22

2009016541

Printed in the United States of America

10 9 8 7 6 5 4 3 2

My love for being a happy woman, and a happy working mother, comes from the love of my life and my daughter, Elisabeth Oriana. This book is dedicated to her and the wonderful spirit of joy she chooses to live with as my ultimate mirror in this lifetime.
Cathy L. Greenberg

This book is dedicated to my husband, Alain, and my beautiful sons, Alexander and Harrison. Your unconditional love and support bring me joy and make me strong. And, to my mother, Caryl Starobin, who was my first role model as a working mom.
Barrett S. Avigdor

Contents

Foreword

Helping working mothers has been my passion and my work for 30 years. As the CEO of Working Mother Media, I've been fortunate to work with many extraordinary women and men who have dedicated themselves to making the lives of working mothers a little easier. Cathy Greenberg and Barrett Avigdor are committed to helping working mothers go beyond coping to find true happiness and joy in their lives.

During our first conversation, they won me over with their science-based approach to what could seem like a very soft issue. Happiness, after all, is not something we normally think of as a health issue or as a component of being a high-performing worker. Many working mothers, consumed with impossibly long to-do lists, think of happiness as a luxury, if they think of it at all. Many would say that they are basically happy with their choices to work and to be a mom. Overall, they love their kids and most love their work. But, on a daily basis, those women will tell you that they are too stressed out and exhausted to fully enjoy their kids or their work. And guilt, the constant companion of many working mothers, will consume any bit of joy that they find.

This book will show you that happiness is a necessity. In order to be your best at work and as a mother, you need to make choices that make you happy. Letting go of guilt is a big part of it too. Cathy and Barrett will convince you that your happiness is essential to the well-being of your family and to maximize your contribution at work. They will also show you how to find happiness—however you define it.

Working mothers have gained many successes over the last few decades. We've earned recognition as an important part of the work force. We've shattered many stereotypes and preconceived notions about what working mothers can and cannot do. This book takes us to the next level. It shows us how to take all the freedom we've won over the last 4 decades and to use it to make the very personal choice to be happy.

Cathy and Barrett have an important message to share with working mothers, their families, and their employers. They provide insights that open your eyes to see your world as full of possibilities. They give you the tools to begin to make your own choices that will get you on the path to a live a life full of joy and happiness.

—Carol Evans
CEO, Working Mother Media

Preface

As you would expect, we each come to this book with different life experiences but a shared vision for the importance of happiness and a strong desire to share that with women all over the world.

Cathy was living the jet-set life traveling the globe as an international business consultant and executive coach for Fortune 500 companies when she hit the "wall of life" hard. It forced her to shift her priorities and refocus or risk losing family, work, and even her life. In addition to being the first female partner hired from the outside at one of the world's top firms, she was the first female executive director to found a leadership institute. Cathy has been fortunate to have been blessed with great mentors and to have co-authored several award-winning books, *Global Leadership: Next Generation* with Marshall Goldsmith, *The Future of Leadership* with Warren Bennis, and most recently *What Happy Companies Know* and *What Happy Women Know* with Dan Baker. She has also been blessed with a wonderful family and, although her parents have passed on, she has a loving daughter and two brothers, both with daughters of their own. All of them continue to teach her how to be truly happy as a woman, a mother, and a professional coach.

Barrett has had a successful career as an international lawyer. A Fulbright scholar to Brazil and a graduate of the University of Chicago Law School, she has been able to combine her legal skills with her love of foreign cultures and travel. With a good work ethic, excellent mentors, and a little luck, she has been able to build a career around her strengths. Despite all that success, she made the unorthodox decision to move from Chicago to Tucson, Arizona, in 2000, when her two sons were very young. That move allowed her to be a full-time mom and a full-time lawyer. It also taught her the importance of having a network of family and friends to help out with the kids when she was traveling. The move was the first big decision she had ever made that was driven by her quest for happiness. It was the best decision as well, as it allowed her to spend far more time with her wonderful sons, Alexander and Harrison, and her devoted husband, Alain. Without them, she could not be a happy working mother.

When we met over a decade ago at a Sunday evening negotiation planning session for an outsourcing deal, we never imagined we would eventually move to the same city far from our roots and combine our love of what we do to create *What Happy Working Mothers Know*. It's a joy to share our stories and those of many others just like you who have dreams and hopes of being all we can be in this lifetime.

We hope you will join us to learn how the new science of happiness can change your life for the better and help you achieve significance and peace as both a woman and a mother, and fulfill whatever role you choose for yourself at home or in the workplace. We would love to hear from you, so please share your ideas, your passion, your comments, and (more important) your joys with us at www.WhatHappyWorkingMothersKnow.com.

In Happiness,
Cathy Greenberg and Barrett Avigdor

Acknowledgments

To write a book about happiness and working mothers requires that many people share their stories, their talents, and their support. We cannot possibly thank each and every one of you by name but we do thank you.

The following deserve a very special mention:

◆ Warren Bennis, Marshall Goldsmith, and Noel Tichy have all been mentors to Cathy and provided moral and intellectual support for this book when we needed them the most.

◆ Joel Stern, Nancy Laben, and Mike Brownell have been mentors to Barrett. Through their enthusiastic support for the book and the opportunities they provided to help her find her ideal life balance, they made this book possible.

◆ A special thanks goes to friends Mark Goulston, Relly Nadler, and Grace Killelea for their enthusiasm for the topic and for their motivating energy during the development stage of the book.

◆ Sincere gratitude to Melissa Winter, chief of staff for Team MO (Michelle Obama) during the election campaign, and to Christie Hefner for the opportunity to meet Melissa and Michelle in Chicago.

◆ Britt van den Berg at Philips Corporation deserves special thanks as a very early supporter of this project.

◆ Alison O'Kelly and Caroline Evans at Mom Corps for so generously posting our survey online, which allowed us to get input from hundreds of women. Honorable mention goes to Angel Johnson, a new mom herself, for organizing the final data.

◆ Larry E. Smith, Sr., divisional manager of Training, and other executives at Wal-Mart Stores, Inc., Bentonville, Arkansas, for creating the opportunity for us to talk with groups of Wal-Mart employees.

◆ Johanna Dillon and Bill Lombardo, both of Bankers Life and Casualty Company. Johanna, director Field Leadership and Management Development, helped to create the exercise on The Will to Be Happy, and Bill, senior director Bankers Learning Network, for his support.

◆ Lauren Lynch, our wonderful editor at John Wiley & Sons, believed in our idea and was invaluable in bringing it to light. Thanks also go to Peter Knapp and Kate Lindsay.

◆ Susan J. Marks for helping us to corral our many ideas into nine coherent chapters.

◆ Mike Drew, our book promoter and consultant, deserves a warm thanks for his patience and staying the course with us.

◆ The very special and extraordinarily successful women whose stories are featured in this book, we thank you for your time, your trust, and your exceptional optimism.

◆ All those great companies that graciously provided us support and allowed us to talk with their happy employees.

◆ Last, but certainly not least, thanks to the hundreds of women who participated in our focus groups and allowed us to interview them. Your candor, your humor, your humility, and your strength inspire us. A special thank you to the women who were part of our focus groups at the Wal-Mart Distribution Centers. We hope you recognize your quotes and your wisdom throughout this book.

Introduction

Motherhood is the most satisfying and powerful job any woman will ever have. As moms we nurture and shape the lives of our children and our families. Fathers play an important role, yet as mothers, we are the CEOs of our families, and just like in the corporate world, we set the tone. The way we feel affects how our family feels.

Watching and nurturing our children as they grow brings us great joy, and many happy moments. Healthy kids, a good job, and a loving spouse or partner, friends, and family all are part of a happy life. True, deep-down lasting happiness is more than being grateful and it's more than the absence of suffering. Happiness is a view of the world. It comes when you align your life to your values, learn to love and forgive yourself and others, and find true joy in the small details of everyday life.

Sometimes working mothers find the joy and fulfillment of raising a child can be overshadowed by the responsibilities of a full- or part-time job. You have the choice, however, to be energized by the balancing act of family and employment demands or to let it drain you. By taking care of your own happiness, you will be better at everything you do, as a mother, a worker, and partner.

Millions of us happily and successfully mix motherhood and a career day in, day out, and our happy, well-adjusted children, close-knit families, and satisfying jobs are living proof. Work plus motherhood is not a zero sum game. They enhance each other.

Guilt is an enemy of happiness. We feel guilty because we believe that we somehow hurt our children by having a job outside of motherhood. We feel guilty when we work fewer hours than our colleagues who don't have child care responsibilities. Society tells us that by working we jeopardize the well-being of our children and the stability of our marriages. We're given the message that we can't have a happy marriage and happy children along with a career. In reality, though, we can, and we do.

If we embrace the abundance in our lives, we can truly enjoy a happiness that endures even through hard times, whether we're hourly employees or top-level executives, whether we're struggling to make ends meet as a single mom or happily entrenched in a partnership relationship.

Happiness is an energy force that makes a positive difference in your life, and in the lives of your kids, your workplace, and your career. This isn't about fixating on instant gratification or demanding that the world be a perfect place. It's about setting the stage to do and be your best for yourself, for those around you, and for the company you work for. A working mom's glass truly is half full, sometimes overflowing, but certainly not half empty.

Right about now you're probably thinking, "Yeah right! I'll have time to get touchy-feely happy and sing 'Kumbayah' in another lifetime, maybe, if I'm lucky." But before you give in to cynicism, consider this quick test of the power of *your* happiness on those around you.

Think of a very happy time in your life, when you felt your best, and felt full of joy. How did you behave? How did you talk to people, and how did they respond? You probably felt that everything seemed to go right and, when there were setbacks, they didn't upset you. If you smiled, others likely returned the smile because happiness is a positive energy force that makes a difference in everyone's lives.

It all starts with your choice to be happy or not. Each of us can choose to be positive in our approach to life, to make the most of what we have, to see all that is good, and to enjoy our work, our families, and our lives. Or, we can opt for the rat race, the exhaustion, the excuses, the guilt, the anguish, the misery, and the self-pity. This is a book of triumph, about helping working mothers look beyond the negative energy that swirls around all of us, and to instead embrace a positive way of being. It's a life-changing shift in focus that can empower you to live a life of joy.

In today's hard-nosed world—especially the numbers-based realm of business and today's tough economic times—it's easy to dismiss happiness as an unimportant luxury and a time-waster that saps our energies and drains bottom lines. Reality, however, is just the opposite. A positive approach positively affects bottom lines, whether in the boardroom, classroom, or at home. And lack of happiness exacts its financial toll.

Consider some of the numbers:

◆ Working mothers have plenty of company. Nearly 25.7 million mothers with children under 18 were part of the U.S. workforce in 2007. That's nearly double the number in 1975, according to estimates from the U.S. Bureau of Labors Statistics and the Census Bureau's monthly Current Population Survey.[1]

◆ U.S. businesses lose more than $300 billion annually due to employee stress as manifested by increased absenteeism, employee turnover, diminished productivity, medical, legal, and insurance expenses, and workers' compensation payments. Put into perspective, that's 10 times the cost of all workplace strikes combined.[2]

◆ A big chunk of that stress, and therefore cost, is a result of less productive working parents worried about what their children are doing after school, according to a 2006 study from the Community, Families, and Work Program at Brandeis University and Catalyst, a leading nonprofit research and advisory organization.[3]

◆ Worker fatigue—more common in women than men—costs employers an estimated $136 billion-plus a year in health-related lost productivity, according to a 2007 study from the American College of Occupational and Environmental Medicine.[4]

What Happy Working Mothers Know is all about how you can be the best mother and best worker possible by investing in your own happiness. You can learn to find happiness no matter where you are in your life, how overwrought, how overwhelmed, or how unhappy you are. Even if you're already happy, you can learn how to make that happiness last even when things don't go smoothly. We'll show you a few simple steps to take, ways to shift your attitudes and approaches, and techniques to find happiness in the life you have rather than the life you wish you had. By realizing your happiness, you'll be a better parent, better spouse, better employee/boss, better person, and feel better about yourself, too.

While on the presidential campaign trail, now-First Lady Michelle Obama summed up what we hope to convey to you in an address to "Women for Obama" in Chicago, Illinois, on July 28, 2008:

> . . . For working families trying to balance jobs and kids and maybe even aging parents of their own, the American Dream can feel like it's slipping away. Over the course of this campaign, I've had the chance to sit down with so many working women across the country. I've talked with mothers struggling to make ends meet because their salaries aren't keeping up with the cost of groceries or the price of gas. I've listened to the moms who are nervous about taking time off to care for a sick child, and the moms-to-be who are scared of getting fired if the boss finds out they're pregnant . . . .This [Women for Obama booklet] is about helping women reclaim their dreams for themselves and their families. It's about giving them a helping hand, not a handout. . .

This isn't a book of technical doublespeak or catchy phrases, complicated jargon, or unrealistic scenarios. Instead *What Happy Working Mothers Know* is stories from and about real people, real experiences, real moms, real jobs, real workplaces, real hardships, real issues, real solutions, and real happiness. We address the science of happiness, too—it's not a manufactured state or the stuff of pipe-dreams, but is based on scientific fact.

Of the approximately 1,000 women we interviewed for this book, the vast majority agree that motherhood makes them better in their jobs. Motherhood, after all, is great leadership training. As CEOs of the family, mothers set the tone, establish the rules, and do every-thing they can to make every member of the family successful. We talk to these working moms about how they run their families, how they cope, how they triumph, and how they've achieved happiness, often despite seemingly insurmountable odds, impossible hardships, and hopeless situations. We talk to their kids, too, who are quick to refute the myths that they're somehow slighted because their moms work.

We'll also show you how to direct your energies to find and create joy in your life and forget about the guilt. It's an obstacle to your happiness as a working mom. No matter how the odds stack up against you, think about the joy you get from the beauty of your daughter's smile. Or the satisfaction you get from a "well done!" from your boss or if a project turns out beautifully. Sure it's a hassle to drag your son to baseball practice rain or shine, but the grin on his face when he gets a base hit is worth the trouble. These small moments of happiness, the little joys and triumphs that we sometimes overlook make up our lives. We'll show you how to find the joy and beauty in the life you have rather that wishing for something different.

Working moms are moms first and foremost. Nearly 81 percent of mothers say mothering is the most important thing they do, according to "The Motherhood Study: Fresh Insights on Mothers' Attitudes and Concerns," a 2005 study for the Institute for American Values.[5]

In *What Happy Working Mothers Know,* we'll discuss the science behind why happiness boosts our personal and business bottom lines. We'll talk to the experts about the power of positive psychology and help you recognize how focusing on what is good in life as opposed to what isn't can transform your life, your job, and your family.

Others have done it, and so can you. A few of the many people who share their stories throughout this book include:

- ◆ **Kim Martin,** president and general manager of WE tv, and mother of two. Despite a boss who discouraged her from pursuing the network's top job, and some self-doubts of her own, she persisted and triumphed. How big a triumph? Her youngest daughter wants her job someday!
- ◆ **Sharon Allen,** mother of two and assistant police chief, Tucson, Arizona, sacrificed the direct path to her career goals to spend more time with her children. She achieved her goals

anyway, crediting "great time-management skills. . . . And I never gave up being a good mother."

◆ Long before she called the White House home, now-First Lady **Michelle Obama** was a career woman whose income helped her family stay afloat. As a mother, too, Obama says she couldn't have done it all without a support system that centers on her own mother's help in raising her two young daughters. "She keeps me and the girls grounded," she says.

◆ **Benita Fitzgerald Mosley** was the first U.S. African-American to win Olympic gold in the 100-meter hurdles. Yet the media all but dismissed her achievement. Instead of resentment, Mosley stood proud and parlayed what she had learned on the field into a highly successful career, motherhood, and life happiness. Today, she's the mother of two and longtime president of Women in Cable Telecommunications. You learn from all your experiences in life, and the experiences get better, she says.

◆ **Yolanda** married at age 16 and had her first child a year after that. Today, 14 years and four children later, she's still happily married and works at the same Wal-Mart distribution center as her husband and extended family. She's the one who sets the tone for her family. "Setting the tone is like changing my shoes. At work, I am the boss. At home, I put on my flip-flops, and I'm laid-back. When I put on my stilettos, I'll dance all night."

The dilemma of finding happiness as a working mother isn't unique to the United States, either. Different cultures face their own sets of problems and circumstances. For this book we talked to more than 1,000 women across the United States, in Brazil, China, Argentina, the Netherlands, Great Britain, France, and beyond—senior executives of global companies, women in middle management, and women who drive forklifts in warehouses. Each of us manages our work and our family in our own way, but the similarities among this diverse group of working mothers are striking. Almost all of us love our work, adore our children, and struggle with busy and often competing schedules, high demands, and the occasional emergency that always seems to land on our shoulders. In these pages, we share our stories, struggles, and hopes to motivate and guide you to your own your unique path to happiness.

Throughout the book we'll also include easy exercises, "Self-Coaching Breaks"—as well as longer exercises at the end of each chapter, "Bottom Lines." These exercises and tools can help you learn to apply the concepts throughout the book. Our goal is to give you the tools to engage your whole brain, help you develop awareness, and learn to perform at your best every day.

What Happy Working Mothers Know also includes the personal stories from mothers who have triumphed over hardships—"A Mother's Story" and "Authentically Happy"—to help you better understand the possibilities for happiness. Their kids share their stories, too. Together these stories will help you better understand yourself, your needs, your wiring, and how to achieve your happiness.

In some cases, we use the real names of mothers, in others we've substituted names or combined stories of individuals to preserve their privacy and the privacy of their children.

Picking up this book is the first step to finding your true happiness. Happiness can be your reality.

We—co-authors Cathy L. Greenberg, Ph.D., and Barrett S. Avigdor, J.D.—are your guides to help you find your happiness. We are both certified executive and personal coaches, and together have 50 years of combined experience in the business world across multiple industries. We are experts in combining the science of happiness with the practical application of a good coach. This book is your pocket personal coach to happiness. It's your access to the information, awareness, and techniques you need to be the best working mother you can be—both at work and at home.

It is our dream to help women achieve their happiness and reclaim their lives as mothers, as women, and as professionals, regardless of their job, income level, or personal struggles. Whether you're a short-order cook or in the C-suite of a Fortune Global 500 company, you're nonetheless the chief executive of your life. One reason we wrote this book is to help working moms who don't have the time or the budget to get the personal or executive coaching they need. Whether you feel the pinch of time or lack of funds, our hope as coaches is to help you and women everywhere—and those who love you or enjoy working with you—perform at your very best. Before any of us can get the support we may need to be our best at work and at home, we need to create awareness of the importance of our overall happiness and the impact it has on our ability to be our best at work and at home.

As a mother, you're charged with helping others find success, too. But you can do that only if you know what it takes for your own success. *What Happy Working Mothers Know* gives you the tools you need and the stories to motivate you.

We hope this book empowers you to find your own happiness because it *is* important.

Chapter 1

Happiness Is Not a Luxury; It's a Necessity

Being a mother is the hardest job of all. It's easier to be a doctor than a mother. Being a mother is a 24/7/365 job forever.

—Victoria, physician and mother of three

As a working mother—no matter your circumstances—happiness is yours for the living, if you choose. Everyone needs happiness, and every one of us can afford and attain it. It's not a luxury reserved only for the wealthy with time and plenty of support.

Happiness is a responsibility and a choice that each of us makes. It's a gift, but not from someone else; instead it comes from within. As working mothers we owe that gift to ourselves, our families, and our jobs. Happiness, after all, helps us to be better at everything we do. Scientific, workplace, and behavioral studies support that finding. Happy working mothers prove it day in and day out.

By happiness, we don't mean sitting around giggling all day or singing feel-good songs. We mean the happiness that allows you to enjoy being your most fulfilled self—whether as a mother, lover, wife, coworker, boss, or all of the above.

Taking a pill or reading a book doesn't make someone suddenly happy, nor is happiness a sometime thing. Happiness starts in the way we view ourselves, our families, our work, and our everyday lives. It's a positive choice each of us can make every day, no matter our circumstances, and it will make a difference in our performance as a mom, in the workplace, and as a wife or a partner.

Happiness Tip: Learn to love yourself as much as you love your friends and family.

How you feel makes a difference to those around you. If you doubt that, try this. One day, act like you are in a great mood. Smile, offer to help people, be cheerful. Play it up but be believable. See how people respond. Most likely, they will ask you questions or share ideas with you. Then try the opposite. Put on a grumpy act. Tighten your face and let your body language say, "don't bother me!". Compare the responses and see how much your mood impacts others and the way they interact with you.

A Mother's Story

Beth, mother of three, works in a Wal-Mart distribution center in the Midwest. She likes her job, and the mood in her family is relaxed and happy. That wasn't always the case. When Beth worked in law enforcement—as a prison guard—she described herself as mean and negative, and that negativity would rub off on her family.

You Deserve Happiness

Happiness is a right of every working mother every day. We all can and should expect to enjoy life, career, relationships, and our kids. Whether we work for financial necessity, fulfillment, or both, we all have the choice of being gratified while balancing work and family or allowing ourselves to get caught up in the rat race. The stresses and strains of everyday pressures—from economics to workplace issues, kids' demands, familial duties, and household responsibilities—enhance our need for happiness. They can also block our happiness if we chose to let them.

Nearly 7 out of 10 working mothers said they believe that they can "have it all" as in motherhood and a successful career, according to a 2007 study from Accenture, (NYSE: ACN), a global management consulting, technology services, and outsourcing company.[1] Looking at more from that online survey of 700 working mothers in mid- to senior-level management positions:

- ◆ Nearly 90 percent of working mothers like working and would want to stay on the job if there were no obstacles to their working full-time, part time, or in a flextime arrangement.
- ◆ More than 74 percent of working mothers are satisfied that their work/life balance is always or most of the time "right."

Finding the right work/life, isn't always easy. For many people, finding the right balance and achieving happiness is a question of adjusting your mind-set, and rethinking some behaviors. Let's look more closely.

What Is Happiness?

*Happiness is the meaning and the purpose of life, the
whole aim and end of human existence.*
—Aristotle, 384 B.C. to 322 B.C.

Happiness means different things to different people. Happiness is the "overall experience of pleasure and meaning," says Tal Ben-Shahar, Ph.D., a psychologist, author of *Happier: Learn the Secrets to Daily Joy and Lasting Fulfillment,* and instructor of a hugely popular happiness course, Positive Psychology, at Harvard University.

The what-happy-working-mothers-know definition of happiness is living a life aligned to your values and knowing how to find joy in simple things. Joy can be as simple as your child's smile or helping an elderly gentleman across the street, or as complex as sealing a particular deal at work, or getting a promotion. Those are all valid examples and provide a fleeting sense of satisfaction. But happiness, as we define it, is a long-term state of mind. Let's examine the reality of what motivates working mothers to choose to lead happy lives long term, and how you to can learn to achieve such a life, too.

Perspectives on Happiness

Each of us defines happiness in our own way. Here's how one group of working mothers, with children ages 8 months to 23 years, answers the question: What is happiness?

- **"Flexibility and balance**," says Lisa, who works part-time from home and has two grown children, ages 23 and 21.
- **"Being a role model; demonstrating that families can do things differently and still be happy,"** says Zoe, mother of two, ages 7 and 11.
- **"Being successful at home and at work,"** says Reveka, mother of a 9-year-old.
- **"Fulfillment as a mother, at work, as a spouse, and personally,"** says Maria, mother of two, ages 15 and 13.
- **"Knowing that others can grow based on my performance—especially so my daughter can see how to work on a team,"** says Elizabeth, mother of an 8-month-old.
- **"I can release control, and I don't have to do it all!"** says Margie, mother of two, ages 16 and 17.
- **"At the end of the day everyone has had a good day and we are pitching in like a team. It's that moment,"** says Sierra, also a mother of two teens.
- **"To me it seems decadent to be soul-searching. Happiness is being satisfied,"** says Susan, mother of four now-grown children.

State of Being

True happiness is a state of being, an approach to living life that generates positive energy for you and those around you at home and at work. Some forward-thinking employers already are recognizing that happy employees make better employees and that happiness is reflected in the bottom line—happiness equals profit. It's the same when it comes to working mothers. We, too, can take many of the lessons from the boardrooms and corporate battlefields and make them work toward our own happiness.

"What you learn in the boardroom, you can apply in the home and in the community and vice versa," says Benita Fitzgerald Mosley, a mother of two and president and CEO of Women in Cable Telecommunications. "It happens seamlessly. You learn from the experiences across your life, and they get better and better," adds the 1984 Olympic gold medalist in track and field. "I have always enjoyed the integration of all these facets in my life that have made me who I am. I love being a daughter, a mother, and a career woman. I have been married for 13 years and have two children. I am very happy doing both roles as a mother and an executive."

Abundance Mentality

Happiness is a state of mind in which we focus on the positive things and the people in our lives—the things and the people we appreciate. As Mosley does, it's embracing the abundance (positive) mentality versus one of scarcity (negativity). It's about drawing on what's good not dwelling on what's not. It's the conscious choice to look beyond the imperfect and learn how to be happy.

Jenny is a single mom, a cancer survivor, a caregiver for her elderly mother, and works full time as a sixth-grade teacher. Yet every morning she wakes up with a positive approach to life. "My son is my pride and joy," she says. "The kids at school can be a hassle, but I love my job, and if I help just one youngster to succeed, it's extremely gratifying. Being a mom and caregiver has made me more understanding and compassionate about the hardships many kids face. Being a teacher, on the other hand, has taught me greater patience with my own son and with my mom."

The "Perfect" Myth

To be happy, you first need to let go of the myth that you need to be perfect to be happy. Barbie is a doll, not a role model, and Debra Barone—the sexy, sassy wife and mother in *Everybody Loves Raymond*, who raises her kids (and her husband) while she deals with difficult in-laws—is a fictional mother. Wonder Woman was a figment of the TV imagination, too. As for that woman in the television commercial who brings home the bacon, fries it up in a pan, and knows how to please her man—needless to say, she doesn't exist. When you stop striving for perfection according to some fictional standard, you can redirect your energy to the things that matter to you.

Happiness is like good health. Without it, you may be alive but you won't be your best at home or at work, and likely neither will those around you. You control your own happiness much like you control your physical fitness. Happy people cultivate certain habits and practices that help them lead happy lives at work and at home—and often despite the trials and tribulations of their lives.

Authentically Happy

If you are a naturally happy person, the inevitable dramas in life will not keep you down for long.

Sue is a longtime working mother, now a working grandmother, and still married to the love of her life (she married at age 18). She's faced her share of hardships, but is happily resilient and always sees the glass as half full.

The Philadelphian recently took in her 3-year-old granddaughter—the child of her divorced son (she and her son fought for full custody and they won)—after having successfully raised her own 20-something son and daughter. Sue takes care of her elderly parents, too. And she loves doing it all, while working a full-time job at a private school.

One of Sue's brothers died of hepatitis at a young age, and her father never recovered from the loss. Sue's mother has always been the heart of the family, just as Sue is to her family that includes Mitch (a successful entrepreneur), daughter Lauren, and son Rick, a postal worker.

Sue loves nice things and so do her kids. Beyond that, though, she has tried to instill good moral and ethical values in her children.

Sue has struggled with weight all her life. At age 45, she had gastric bypass surgery, which almost killed her. But today she is the poster child for successful weight loss while battling diabetes, too.

Despite her hardships, Sue never gives up and always looks for the silver lining. She loves being the working "grandma" and would probably raise granddaughter Bella's kids, too, given the chance. Sue also helps her daughter, Lauren, by employing her at the school when she is between jobs. Despite such a schedule, Sue takes time for herself one day a week.

Sue is the consummate mother. She's happy, too, and that's what really matters.

Your Own "Perfect"

As human beings, each of us sets the parameters for our own happiness. **Happiness is** "self-actualization, feeling satisfied with one's accomplishments, having reached the goals you set for yourself financially, emotionally, and professionally," says Kathy, a wife and working mother of two in Shanghai, China.

Happiness is "essential for all of us. It's what gets you up every day. It's ridiculous to say, 'I don't have time to be happy,'" says Julie, a CPA in Tucson, Arizona, and mother of two teenagers, 14 and 17.

Happiness is "doing right by yourself so you are healthy, fit, and mentally awake. Doing right by your family. Doing right by society," says Nancy Laben, 46, Chicago-based deputy general counsel for Accenture and mother of two children, ages 16 and 14. "I think of it as concentric circles. I am the small circle in the middle. What makes me happy? Making my daughter happy and seeing her delight in finding something just right. Volunteering is a happy moment. Taking time to think about what this life means is a happy moment. Happiness is made up of drops of time," says Laben.

Happiness is "a sense of the possible," says Robin, 44, mother of three (ages 10, 12, and 14), and executive director of a nonprofit. "You feel that things are possible. You feel bouncy. You want to pass it on."

Although these women may be in different places geographically, economically, and personally, they all have the goal of happiness in common and have figured out what it takes to reach that goal. They know what they want, what matters, and they have chosen to pursue it.

Foundation for Your Happiness

Ask yourself the following questions, and be honest in your answers:

- Do I have the foundation for my own happiness?
- Do the people in my life contribute to my happiness?
  - Do my family members/relationships support my happiness?
  - Do my coworkers support my happiness?
  - Do my friends support my happiness?
- If the answer to any of these questions is "no," have you told them what you need them to do (stop doing) in order to support your happiness?
  - If not, why not?
  - If so, why haven't they done it?
- What kind of additional support do I need to be happy?
  - Are these things, people, time, energy, money, or something else?
  - How can I get them if I do not have them?
  - Can I do this myself or do I need help?
  - Is the help related to time, energy, or money?
- What next steps do I need to take to make my foundation for happiness a success?

Wants, Needs, and Becoming Better

Working moms love what they do, whether happiness is on their minds or not. In fact, 78 percent of mothers say they're "fulfilled," according to "What Moms Want,"[1] a survey from Working Mother Media (www .workingmother.com), publishers of the *Working Mother* magazine. Balance is a challenge, *Working Mother* reports. "But moms are making it work. That's not to say there aren't a lot of challenges and stress—there are—but our survey shows that moms are NOT giving up."

Ambitions are important to working moms, too. In the survey, 62 percent of women describe themselves as "very ambitious."

Self-Coaching Break: What Matters to You

(Money, Time, and Energy)

Happy people align their time to their values. This exercise will help you see where your time and values align and where they do not.

- List those values in life that have meaning to you. (See Figure 1.1A.)
- List each value separately.
- Pick the top five for immediate focus and review.
- Rank them in order of importance.
- List the percentage of money you spend on these values using 100 percent of your funds as a base.
- List the number of minutes or hours per week you devote to this value, then fill in the chart using a percentage of your overall time based on an average work week.
- List the amount of energy you invest in this value as positive (+) or negative (−) (e.g. it gives you a positive or negative feeling when you do it).
- Use the template to track your answers and demonstrate your awareness.

(continued)

FIGURE **1.1A**   What Matters to You

Value (in order of importance before completing this exercise)	% of money you spend on it each week	Number of hours/ minutes you spend on it as a percentage of time each work week	Amount of energy + or –	Re-order by importance after completing this exercise

◆ When completed, you should have a record of how your use of money, time, and energy match your values (See Figure 1.1B). If they are not aligned, consider changes you can make to bring them into alignment, and re-order your values as needed.

FIGURE **1.1B**

What Matters To Me	Money	Time	Energy
• Raising healthy, balanced children	33%	15 hrs driving kids	Negative (−)
• Doing interesting/useful work	5%	60 hours	Positive (+)
• Saving for retirement and job loss	33%	15 min planning	Negative (−)
• Leisure time (exercise, movies)	20%	5 hours exercising	Positive (+)
• Maintaining relationships	5%	2 hours	Positive (+)
• Contributing to community	1%	0 hours	Negative (−)
• Other	3%	5–10 hours	Positive (+)

On-the-Job Training

Mothers, as the CEO and management of their families, set the tone and goals for their families just as at the workplace where the CEO sets tone and management goals for the company. Many working mothers are ambitious and that isn't surprising considering motherhood is good training ground for coping with the trials, tribulations, and challenges of the workplace. Motherhood makes women more effective in the workplace, too. "It gives you the experience of being totally in charge and you realize how capable you are," says Dee Dee Myers, mother of two, former White House press secretary for President Bill Clinton (the first woman to ever be appointed to that position), political analyst and commentator, contributing editor to *Vanity Fair*, and author of *Why Women Should Rule the World* (www .deedeemyers.org).

As mothers, we have empowering information and experience, Myers adds. "We need to get women to believe that even in work circumstances, they can also be in charge. You also learn to trust your intuition more when you are a mother. Intuition is real and is a valuable tool. You should trust that voice. We should not be defensive about it," adds Myers.

PROGRAMMED WIRING

Recognizing our power and strengths as women isn't always the way we're programmed. We're often raised to take a backseat to others' happiness, to please everyone else first. Society does little to dissuade us of that or to help working mothers cope with the demands of mixing work and family. That same society—worldwide, in varying degrees—often frowns on working moms. Despite some high-profile exceptions, the business world doesn't make it much easier.

Heather, mother of three—ages 7, 11, and 14—and a state senator, is a happy working mother today. That wasn't always the case. She consciously allowed her own happiness to take a backseat to that of her family's and stayed home full-time with her kids for six years. Although she adored being home with her kids, Heather longed to contribute to the world in other ways. Once her youngest started school, Heather says she felt she could go back to work full time to gain the fulfillment she was lacking.

Individuals like Heather and Dee Dee Myers and others create their own happiness. As mothers and businesswomen, they've learned the behaviors that facilitate their happiness. As a working mother, you can transform your life even if you're not naturally happy. That's what Heather did. Even her desire to be a happy stay-at-home mom—the force of her will for happiness—wasn't enough to turn her life toward happiness. Instead, Heather says, "It's about knowing what makes you happy and building time in your life for those things. You need to pay attention to the small things that make you happy . . . to treat yourself to the things you enjoy."

In Heather's case, those happiness triggers include being back at work, feeling needed, having a role in something bigger than herself, and feeling purposeful.

"I'm a glass half-full person," says attorney Laben. To achieve her positive outlook she learned how to recognize and appreciate moments of happiness. "It's a life skill," says Laben. "It's part of parenting."

What are *your* happiness triggers? What is it that lifts your spirit and helps you embrace the abundance mentality? Let's paint a picture in your mind of all that is good in your life. Create a happier view of your life (Figure 1.2), and then take the Abundance Audit Self-Assessment (Figure 1.3).

Self-Coaching Break

Look at your life as a window and fill it in with the people and places in your life that contribute to your happiness. Use this window to view your happy life and make changes as needed. You can put in photos or the names of people and places. You can even post this on your Facebook page if you like.

Now, take the abundance Audit. Be candid and honest. Even little things that are good can and do add up.

FIGURE **1.2**   Creating a Happier Life View

FIGURE **1.3**   Abundance Audit Self-Assessment

Background:

As working mothers we are faced with time constraints. As a result, we become focused on the negative rather than the positive. An example might include how we view our achievements or those around us, a loved one, like our partner or our children. Did we look at what is working, what went right or what might not have gone as well as expected? Are we realistic with our schedule, planning for activities, tasks at work, or expectations of ourselves and others? Applying focus and attention to the list of words below will help you understand what if any adjustments might be needed to help you maintain or achieve a higher Mentality of Abundance that is critical to better health, emotional wellness, and managing the talent you have as both a mother and in your career.

Directions:

Please read the statements below to help you understand the answers you may apply in rating yourself in Part I.

Think about how effective you are applying an Abundance Mentality using these statements.

Part I. On a scale of 1 to 10 (10=very strong, 5=ok, 1=very weak), rate or assess yourself in the areas below for Abundance in both your professional and your

(continued)

personal life. (Please read the definitions listed below before completing the scale).

Establishing Rapport	**Creating a personal connection or common ground with someone to make it more comfortable to have a conversation.**
Listening	**Shifting to deeper levels of listening where attention is fully on the other person, and being conscious of the impact of that listening**
Developing Self-Awareness	**Understanding and articulating your own perspectives, reactions, and assumptions to better understand the "lenses" through which you view the world.**
Demonstrating Empathy	**Accepting and valuing another person's perspective and showing a genuine interest in understanding the other person.**
Asking Questions/ Inquiring	**Using guiding questions to help someone think through an issue of making a decision. Allowing the person to solve the problem him/herself.**
Enabling	**Encouraging someone to fully use gifts and talents in creative ways by being excited about his or her actions and progress and pointing to underlying shifts and growth.**
Collaboratively Problem Solving	**Finding value in someone's ideas and building on them to explore issues and jointly create solutions.**
Providing and Receiving Feedback	**Highlighting the impact of current behaviors and identifying new behaviors and actions that improve performance.**

1. Establishing Rapport

1	2	3	4	5	6	7	8	9	10

2. Listening

1	2	3	4	5	6	7	8	9	10

3. Developing Self-Awareness

| 1 | 2 | 3 | 4 | 5 | 6 | 7 | 8 | 9 | 10 |

4. Demonstrating Empathy

| 1 | 2 | 3 | 4 | 5 | 6 | 7 | 8 | 9 | 10 |

5. Asking Questions/Inquiring

| 1 | 2 | 3 | 4 | 5 | 6 | 7 | 8 | 9 | 10 |

6. Enabling

| 1 | 2 | 3 | 4 | 5 | 6 | 7 | 8 | 9 | 10 |

7. Collaborative Problem Solving

| 1 | 2 | 3 | 4 | 5 | 6 | 7 | 8 | 9 | 10 |

8. Providing and Receiving Feedback

| 1 | 2 | 3 | 4 | 5 | 6 | 7 | 8 | 9 | 10 |

Look at the total number of times you circled a particular number (1-10) above. Using the overall scale below, circle the number that most closely corresponds to those numbers above. If you circled mostly 8-10 above, you are most likely having good results and demonstrate a highly effective Mentality of Abundance. If you circled mostly 4-7, you are probably doing well and are moderately effective with a Mentality of Abundance. If you circled 1-3 you are probably not as effective as you could be using and applying a higher level Mentality of Abundance. By examining some key obstacles in Part II below, you can begin to develop more of these skills

Part II. What are 3-5 key obstacles in your life to building and exercising an Abundance Mentality? (e.g., no time, haven't had good role models and/or training, leadership in my firm doesn't seem to value these skills, my family expects me to make it all work, etc.) Continue with Part III.

1.

2.

3.

4.

5.

(*continued*)

Part III. List 5-10 adjectives to describe Abundance in both your professional and personal life (e.g., my talents, skills, strengths, good at relationships, problem solver, excellent communicator, I understand my children, people confide in me, I am trustworthy, quick learner, self-motivated, etc.). This section will help you include more "words" or phrases that will enable you to apply more Abundance in your life. Keeping this list in a visible place can help you simulate your Abundance Mentality (e.g., on a screen saver, on your cell phone next to names of "energizing" people, include them with photos for your desktop, car, or gym locker).

1.   6.

2.   7.

3.   8.

4.   9.

5.   10.

Part IV. What do you hope to gain by demonstrating an appreciation for Abundance?

• Personally:

  ◦ For you

  ◦ For your family

• Professionally:

  ◦ For you

  ◦ For your team/firm/industry

Why Bother with Happiness?

The presence of happiness changes the landscape wherever you are and in whatever you do. If you're happy, your personal relationships are more upbeat, your children more energized, and your work more improved. The absence of happiness, on the other hand, exacts a toll on everyone around you and all you do.

A Working Mother's Wisdom

Paradoxically, a diagnosis of cancer often creates more happiness in the lives of cancer patients because they are forced to drop the trivial irritants. The change of perspective, emphasizing the preciousness of life, can actually make them happier. It enhances their ability to appreciate joy more accurately.

Loss can often help you experience joy. When you go to the end of the pain continuum, you appreciate the other end of the spectrum—which is joy.

—Victoria, M.D., and mother of three

In the Workplace

Happiness equals profit in the workplace. If the costs of health care decrease, if employees take fewer sick days (including "mental health" days), and if the cost of employee turnover drops, companies decrease their expenses and increase their overall profit. That's because when people work in a positive environment, they're less stressed. Low stress means the different parts of the brain—the amygdala and the frontal cortex (we'll talk more about them in the next chapter)—can work together optimally to make well-reasoned, ethical decisions. Just as stress causes high blood pressure and other physical health symptoms, low stress levels can reduce those symptoms, and the result is less employee time out for sickness.[2]

Fostering happy employees is the single greatest transformation a company can undergo to retain talent, improve its competitive position, and increase its top line revenue. It also has the potential to drastically reduce stress and medical-related workplace costs (and bottom lines in the process). Consider a few numbers on the cost of *un*happiness in the workplace:

◆ Employee stress costs U.S. businesses more than $300 billion annually from increased absenteeism, employee turnover, diminished productivity, and medical and legal costs.[3]

◆ As many as 2.5 million working parents are less productive employees because they're worried about what their children are doing after school, according to a 2006 study from the Community, Families, and Work Program at Brandeis University and Catalyst, a leading nonprofit research and advisory organization. "Our findings show that [parental worry about kids after school] can be very toxic to employee attitudes, work performance, and well-being," says Karen Gareis, a social psychologist at the Community, Families, and Work Program, and lead researcher on the study.[4]

◆ Worker fatigue—more common in women than men—affects nearly 40 percent of U.S. workers and costs employers an estimated $136 billion-plus a year in health-related lost productivity, according to a 2007 study from the American College of Occupational and Environmental Medicine.[5]

Cost of Unhappiness in Workplace = Cost of Health Benefits + Number of Sick Days + Cost of Replacing Lost Talent

Happy Employees = Productive Employees

"If employees feel happy about what they are doing, they become more committed and thus complete their tasks more efficiently and to a higher standard," reports iOpener, a consulting firm in the United Kingdom, the Netherlands, and South Africa. iOpener was co-founded by Jess Pryce Jones, one of two working mothers with the purpose of helping companies improve their happiness quotient and bottom lines. "There is a particularly strong established correlation between happiness and productivity," iOpener reports (www.iopener.co.uk/index. php). "Business has inherently always been about success, and happiness was assumed to be a welcome but unnecessary by-product. However, as plenty of successful people would testify, success is not the same as happiness. We agree with this in that success alone does not lead to long-term business commitment, loyalty, or motivation, whereas being happy at work *does.*"[6]

Employee engagement—the emotional connection people have to their work or their level of commitment to it—is a strong indicator of a successful business. According to studies done by Hewitt Associates, high-performing companies are those with employee engagement of 60 percent or higher.[7] Happy employees are highly engaged employees. So, for a business to be considered a high performer in its industry, it needs happy and engaged workers.

Top executive coaches around the world work with all types and sizes of companies, government and private organizations, and even the military on how to foster a positive or happy approach everyday and how to motivate employees to higher performance levels in the process.

At Home

A working mother's happiness makes a difference on the home front, too. Just ask a child or partner of a working mother and they'll tell you. Says Matt, teenaged son of a working mom: "You can definitely tell if Mom had a bad day at work. I know I need to give her space before I ask for anything or to go anywhere."

Work energizes Britt van den Berg, director of Global Diversity and Inclusion/Talent Recruitment, Philips Corporation, and a full-time working mother of a 13-month-old. "It's energy I give back to my daughter," she says. Britt, her partner, and their daughter live in Holland, a place where women typically only work part-time after having children. After her daughter was born, Britt says she felt very somber and overwhelmed by the responsibility of caring for another human being even though her partner was there to help. The prospect of going back to work, however, lifted Britt's spirits. "I'm a better mother because I work. I also feel very responsible for my job because I have a child to support," she says.

I am the barometer, and I set the mood for the family. . . . When I'm grumpy, everyone is on eggshells.
—Jill, clinical nurse specialist, mother of three

Work makes Tatiana happy, too, and has a positive influence on her mothering. She's a mother of three—a daughter, 12, and twin sons, 10—happily married to a lawyer, and living in Great Britain. "Managing children is harder than managing a team at work," she says. "Motherhood makes me better at multitasking and gives me a new perspective. I don't stress over the little things," Tatiana says.

At the same time, her work skills make her a better mother, too, she says. Negotiation training, for example, has helped her manage the kids, motivating them, building their self-esteem, and recognizing their accomplishments. "My happiness is important to my family. It gives me more energy to spend with them and sets the tone for family."

Tatiana and Britt aren't alone in feeling that working makes them better mothers and vice versa. That's a common theme among mothers in the workplace, whether they drive a forklift truck in a warehouse or steer giant corporations.

Motherhood has changed work for Dee Dee Myers, too. "I'm better at getting to win/win," she says. "I did not appreciate before how important it is for everyone to be happy. I realize now it's important for people to feel they've been heard. I'm better at setting boundaries. My world view has changed somewhat, too. I always thought it was important for women to be involved in all aspects of public life. I feel that way even more now . . . I have a broader view of what it means to have meaningful work."

Your Happiness: Luxury or Not?

Happiness is a necessity, says Diana, 51, adjunct professor of law at the University of Arizona, wife, and mother of a 17-year-old. "You make the necessary changes to be happy. This is the only life we have, so we had better enjoy it."

Diana understands that happiness is self-awareness—each of us understanding our needs; self-care (making sure our needs are met), and self-love (learning to accept ourselves for who we are—imperfections and all), and living in accordance with our values.

Happiness is a part of the life you make for yourself, agrees Debra, a licensed therapist, commodities trader, and divorced mother of two sons whom she co-parents with her ex-husband. "My happiness is paramount to my children . . . . If I act like a victim, that's not healthy. I model boundaries and limits, and show that happiness is not something you have to wait to get. You should be happy now—every day . . . . If I'm miserable, that will trickle down to the boys."

Not all working mothers have learned to be that self-aware, to accept who they are, and to live their values. It's often easier to dwell on the negative especially when, as a working mother, you're stretched thin. True happiness requires not only appreciating the good parts of your life but also this self-awareness of your needs and how to make sure those needs are met. It's not solely about meeting the needs of your kids and your family.

Mosley, of Women in Cable Telecommunications, became the first African-American woman to win Olympic gold when she won the 100-meter hurdles at the 1984 Olympics. At the time, track sensation Mary Decker was the favorite to win the 3,000 meters, but collided with another runner and fell, so did not win in her event. Despite Mosley's landmark victory, the media spotlight focused on Decker's loss. Rather than feel bitter or resentful, Mosley focused on her magnificent accomplishment and walked away from the experience to succeed as a mother, wife, and businesswoman. Recalls Mosley:

"I remember that day in 1984 . . . all the media attention was on Mary Decker's falling, not about Benita Fitzgerald (Mosley), the first African-American woman to win the U.S. gold medal in the 100-meter hurdles track and field event. After winning the gold, I was escorted to the press tent in Los Angeles for the media/press interviews. The tent was massive, like a wedding tent, and it was buzzing with cameras and crews from all around the world. When I arrived the press just looked at me and then looked over my shoulder—past me. . . . They were intent on waiting for Mary and getting the story of the day, how Mary Decker lost the 3,000-meter gold medal.

"I could have been regretful about the media coverage, but I was not. To this day I believe I was blessed to have my day in the sun, and if I had put all my eggs in that one little basket—my win at the 1984 Olympics—it would have probably made me very upset. But I went on with my life.

"I recall standing on the victory stand and seeing my parents' pride, and the joy of sleeping with my gold medal that night—going to sleep and knowing I had reached my goal in just 12.84 seconds. The media situation was disappointing, but there have been so many wonderful blessings in my life since that day . . . . If I had a chip on my shoulder, I would have been an angry, unsuccessful individual for the rest of my life. I chose to be happy and proud of my achievement and to represent my hometown of Dale City, Virginia."

Such is the power of thinking in terms of the abundance in your life—all that is good—as opposed to all that is not. Mosley recognized then and now, 25 years later, that true happiness yields much greater rewards than its opposite, and that it was and is well worth the effort to achieve and sustain that happiness.

Achieving Your Own Happiness

Like Mosley and other women, you, too, can mobilize your thoughts, feelings, and approach to life with happiness as the goal. Plenty of temptations and roadblocks stand in the way of your goal. We'll talk more about many of them in later chapters. But each is surmountable with the right tools, techniques, and support systems. If you're not naturally happy, we'll help you learn how to modify your behavior. This is change management on steroids. It's Six Sigma applied to your own life. You can learn to identify and improve the positive qualities that support a happier life, and by doing so, help decrease your level of negative emotions in the process that is your life.

"Happiness is an inside job," says Lisa Kamen, a mother and founder of the What Is Your Happiness project and an award-winning filmmaker. She shares her perspective on happiness globally in her documentary, "The H-Factor: Where Is Your Heart."[8]

It will take time to find your own happiness. Think of the abundance in your life whenever that wave of "overwhelmed-ism" gets ready to swamp you. Take time to talk to your kids, tune out the negativity around you, turn off the TV, breathe deeply, and then start again on your quest to happiness. You can do it.

Living the Dream

We all have dreams. Often they begin when we are children with fantasies of adventure or wealth or fame. We're never too old to dream, either, and to work toward achieving our dreams. Even if a dream is only that, the pursuit of that dream can provide great joy. The path toward the dream also may provide new opportunities you otherwise could not see.

Sometimes, however, we forget that to achieve a dream, it must be grounded in reality. The reality of being in relationships with your children with other adults is that you need to nourish them with your time. You also need to allow time for yourself to re-energize.

Many women dream of achieving certain milestones in their careers while, at the same time, having a spouse and raising children. And why not? In today's cyber-world people can work from anywhere. You can live on a mountaintop in Idaho and telecommute to New York every morning if you like. It's important, though, that the dream be set at a realistic pace and that it includes time for everything—time with your spouse, time with your children, time with your friends, and time for you. Otherwise, you may get to the top—whatever that top happens to be—and discover that all you had envisioned simply isn't so.

> *Move over, diamonds; happiness is a girl's best friend.*
> —Cathy Greenberg

Follow Your Dream

While following your dreams, take into account all of the elements that comprise a happy life: work, family, life, friends, relaxation, exercise, and the freedom to grow and change.

(*continued*)

Ask yourself the following questions; listen to your inner coach, be positive with yourself; and help yourself see how you can achieve the dream.

◆ What is the grandest possible dream you have for yourself at this time?
◆ How long do you think it will take to achieve the dream?
◆ Who will you need to be successful (family, friends, business partners, or networks of talent or people)?
◆ What skills, capabilities, experiences, or competencies will you need to be successful? How will you get the skills that you do not yet have?
◆ Who is most excited to see you live this dream (you, your family, your friends, or colleagues)?
◆ What will most enable your success (your knowledge, networking with others, financial assets, time)? How can you get those resources?
◆ Who needs to be a part of your success for you to feel you have truly achieved the dream (only you, your family, friends and colleagues, others)?
◆ What obstacles, if any, do you need to be aware of when planning to achieve your dream? How can you overcome those obstacles?
◆ What are you willing to give up to achieve your dream (leisure time, money, security, other)?
◆ How will you know when you have reached your goal? What milestones will you have passed in the process?

That's a lot of questions, but we hope your answers to them will help you direct your energies toward the right dream with an appropriate time frame in mind. Carefully understanding your responses will help you remain true to yourself, your values, and your motivations, and ultimately will keep you on the path to success you have charted for yourself today and in the future.

True happiness springs from honesty with yourself. Making the best choices for you in key elements of your plan is an essential part of achieving your own happiness with no regrets.

> *Deciding what matters the most to you is vital, so take the time to listen to your own inner voice is extremely important—otherwise you might miss your own message.*
>
> —Sherry Brennan, mother, and vice president, sales strategy & development, Fox Cable Networks

Bottom Lines: Exercises to Try

WRITE YOUR HAPPY STORY

Take a few minutes to write down a happy story about you. It can have happened a. nytime in your life. Use the story to remind yourself of when you felt your best and modeled the kind of happiness you would like to feel often.

MAKING CHOICES

Ask yourself these questions:

- What do I need to know about myself as a mother and a worker to be able to make the best choices for me?
- Will my happiness be affected by these choices and how?
- Will the choices I make have a long-term or a short-term impact and how?
- Can I redirect my choice if it does not work for me?

(*continued*)

- ◆ Who can help me with this choice?
- ◆ What can I do to make the choice work for both my family and my work?
- ◆ What future choices will this choice affect?

Knowing yourself is critical to your happiness. Taking the time to understand yourself, your values and what is important to you as you think about your happiest life is vital. Making the right choices for your happiness is essential for creating a long-term plan and a strong foundation for your own happiness.

Chapter 2

The Science of Happiness

What a great gift to be able to share with the world. We can be women and do it just as well or even better without having to become men.
—Genevieve Bos, *PINK* magazine co-founder

Happiness is different for everyone. What gratifies you or makes you happy evokes a different reaction from your neighbor or niece or brother or the shopkeeper down the street. That doesn't mean happiness is arbitrary. It's not, and it can be scientifically measured. The triggers for happiness can vary between men and women. Widely accepted research even shows a genetic disposition of certain people to be happier than others. There isn't a happiness gene that we know of. But one thing is certain: As individuals, we all influence our own happiness.

Personal mastery: Heightened self-awareness of your behaviors, motivations, and competencies, along with the emotional intelligence to monitor and manage your emotional states.[1]
—Goldsmith, Greenberg, Robertson, and Huchan, *Global Leadership: Next Generation*

The science of happiness, including the application of positive psychology, has found its way into boardrooms as companies realize that happy employees are more productive and more creative than their unhappy counterparts. Executive and life coaches work with clients worldwide to help them learn to recognize and understand their strengths and weaknesses and how to thrive in their environments. You, too, can learn how to use scientific findings on happiness to boost your personal bottom line. You can develop self-awareness—an understanding of your behaviors, motivations, and competencies—and then learn how to manage your emotional intelligence to your advantage. You will learn to do that with the help of information and exercises in this book. Read on.

First, though, let's take a step back to understand the science of happiness and why and how humans react to certain things—whether directed toward themselves, their family members, fellow workers, friends, or even total strangers. We'll also show how such reactions and connections relate to your joy and fulfillment as a working mother. Knowing what's really happening and why is a first step toward learning to make the choices that will lead you to your happiness.

It's in Your Makeup

In 1996, University of Minnesota professor of psychology David Lykken and associate professor Auke Tellegen concluded that genetics play a big role in individual happiness.

They based their landmark finding on years of studying identical twins who had been reared apart. Their research showed that everyone is born with a happiness "set point," a predisposition to happiness or not. It's similar to our set point or predisposed tendency toward a particular weight—when we say that person is "naturally" skinny or heavy or solid. A heavy weight set point doesn't mean a person absolutely has to be heavy, nor does a low happiness set point mean that a person cannot be happy. A set point does, however, genetically give you a 50 percent chance of turning out a particular way, and in the absence of other forces—external or internal—you'll likely end up on that side of the scale.[2]

Several years after Lykken released his happiness study, he followed up with *Happiness: The Nature and Nurture of Joy and Contentment*, a book that discussed how everyone, no matter their happiness set point, can consciously raise their level of happiness. If your genes are not programmed for happiness, you are not necessarily destined to a life of unhappiness. "I wanted people to know that happiness is genetically influenced but it is not fixed," Lykken says. "Happiness is a lake upon which each of us sails our own personal boat. While the standard water level is determined by genetics, it will rise and fall depending on what's going on in a person's life, always returning to baseline in a fairly short while whether he or she wins the lottery or loses the house to a hurricane."[3]

Sonja Lyubomirsky, Ph.D., an associate professor of psychology at the University of California, Riverside, and author of *The How of Happiness* (Penguin), offers a slightly different model of happiness. She developed it with Ken Sheldon of the University of Missouri and David Schkade from the University of California, San Diego. Their model also calls for the 50 percent set point for happiness, then breaks the remaining 50 percent into 10 percent attributed to differences in people's circumstances—financial, health, and physical situations, for example—with the remaining 40 percent available to each of us to mold and change.[4]

Appreciation Counts

Research has shown that appreciation is at the core of an individual's happiness.

- Positive attitude in heart patients increases survival by 20 percent after 11 years.
- Positive talk by couples reduces stress by 15 percent; negative talk increases stress by 48 percent.
- Appreciation reduces physical symptoms and medications, improves hormone balance, and increases production of antibodies.
- Appreciation syncs heart and mind, improves auditory discrimination, spatial awareness, and short- and long-term memory.
- Thoughts and even subtle emotions influence the activity and the balance of the autonomic nervous system, which

(continued)

interacts with our digestive, cardiovascular, immune, and hormonal systems.

◆ Negative reactions create disorder and imbalance in the autonomic nervous system.

◆ Positive feelings like appreciation create increased order and balance in the autonomic nervous system, which results in increased hormonal and immune system balance, and more efficient brain function.

Source: What Happy Companies Know, by Dan Baker, Ph.D., Cathy Greenberg, Ph.D., Collins Hemingway (Pearson Education, 2006); The HeartMath Institute (www.heartmath.org).

According to that model of happiness, when people are surveyed one year after a major life event such as winning the lottery or sustaining injuries in a car crash, they tend to be about as happy as they were before the major event. "Major boosts or dips in our happiness level due to life circumstances tend to be short-lived. We adapt to our life circumstances," their study says. "So what, if anything, can produce a lasting change in our happiness? The answer lies in the final component of the model, the intentional activities we engage in."

As Lykken puts it, if people truly want to overcome their genes and build a happy life, they need to find something useful and enjoyable to do with their time. "I'd suggest people sit down now and take an honest, careful inventory of ways they do things that interfere with their happiness," says Lykken. "Then make up their mind that they're going to stop making troughs in their happiness lake and start making waves."

Happiness Equation

Genetics aside, each of us can help influence our happiness by making good choices. Psychologist Jonathan Haidt even developed a formula for how people can be happier. He's an associate professor of psychology at the University of Virginia and author of *The Happiness Hypothesis* (Basic, 2005). His formula recognized the ability we all have to influence that nonpredisposed 50 percent of our personal happiness equation.

HAIDT'S FORMULA

Level of happiness = set point + current conditions
+ voluntary activities

or

$$H = S + C + V$$

Breaking down his equation:

H = level of happiness overall.
S = set point for happiness based on genetic disposition.
C = current conditions, such as financial stability, living environment, or health.
V = voluntary activities, where and how you choose to spend your time.

If you're not as happy as you would like, Haidt's formula suggests the solution is to focus on those voluntary activities (V) that you can control and making changes in your current situation (C) to increase your happiness (H).

Another way to use the formula to boost your happiness bottom line:

Increase V (voluntary activities) + C (current conditions) to maximize and override S (set point) = greater H (happiness).

If mathematical-like formulas are not your thing, think about this in terms of your life and the influences around you. Think back on different times in your life; you were probably happiest when you felt safe, had enough money, and were surrounded by people you trusted. When any of those elements was missing, you probably felt less than happy. Who you spend time with, what you do, and how you do it affect your happiness level. When you become aware of which people and activities boost your happiness and which detract from it, you can make deliberate choices that will increase your happiness level. When you are happy, you are at your best, at home and at work.

Remember Olympic gold-medalist Benita Fitzgerald Mosley in Chapter 1? She actually won the race but the media did not seem to care about that as much as they did about her teammate's loss (that was her C, current situation). Instead of protesting, she chose to celebrate her extraordinary accomplishment rather than lament the lack of attention by the press (V, her voluntary activities), and walked away with happiness (H).

Happiness Tip: Life happens. What you choose to focus on becomes your experience. Focus on the positive.

Think about working grandmother Sue, also from the previous chapter. What makes her happy is likely a far cry from what many other working moms would enjoy, but it's what works and brings her great joy. Sue's S (set point), combines with her V (voluntary activities—including taking care of her family and extended family) plus C (the current situation—the everyday trials and tribulations she faces) to equal her H (happiness).

Female/Male Differences

Science also shows us that aspects of happiness are gender specific. Women are different from men in how they react to things. Likely each of us at one time or another has been perplexed by the actions of a male co-worker, a partner, or a spouse—and vice versa. We may have questioned how or why that person acted a certain way or reached a particular conclusion. The answer generally lies in the fact that brains are not unisex. Male and female brains differ.

Some of the differences, according to Louann Brizendine, M.D., a neuropsychiatrist, director of the University of California/San Francisco Women's and Teen Girls' Mood and Hormone Clinic, and author of *The Female Brain* (Broadway, 2006), include:

- Neurons in the female brain make more connections in areas governing communication and emotion.
- Neurons in the male brain concentrate more on areas governing sex and aggression.
- Women have 11 percent more neurons in their brains for language and hearing.
- The prefrontal cortex, the portion of the brain responsible for self-control, is larger and matures earlier in women. That's one reason women tend to be more patient than men.
- The amygdala portion of the brain, where fear and aggression originate, is smaller in women, which makes them less likely to take physical risks.
- The space allotted to sex drive in a female brain is smaller than in a male brain.
- The hippocampus, the part of the brain responsible for emotional memory, is larger and more active in females, which is why they remember emotional events in greater detail.

EMOTIONAL DIFFERENCES

Emotional responses of men and women vary, too. Men spend more time on the pursuit of power, status, and things; and women focus on relationships, cooperation, and communication.

Some of those widely documented differences include:

- Women appear to vacillate between happiness and sadness more quickly than men.
- Women experience two to four times more depression than men.
- Women experience more emotion (except anger) than men.
- Women report more positive emotion more frequently and more intensely.
- Women's brains devote more space to emotion and memory.

What this indicates is that women have tremendous potential to develop acute self-awareness and overcome the negative in their lives—whether adversity or emotion, external or internal—to create and embrace joy. The female memory has stored away happiness messages of contentment and joy no matter how dire one's personal circumstances or how buried one's self-love. It's simply a matter of learning the techniques to unlock those memories for the benefit of personal happiness.

DIFFERENT STRESS RESPONSES

For generations, the human response—male and female—to stress typically has been characterized by science as "fight or flight." More recently, landmark research at the University of California/Los Angeles reveals that the female makeup, unlike that of the male, often leads us to "tend and befriend" instead. Under stress, females release the hormone oxytocin, which arouses our nurturing instinct and encourages us to gather with other females. The more we nurture and join with other female friends, researchers say, the more oxytocin is released and the calmer we become. Apparently estrogen enhances the tend-and-befriend reaction.[5]

This helps explain why, when we're stressed, we often feel better after we talk to a girlfriend or our mom or another woman we're close with. From a scientific point of view, researchers say it's in our makeup to join with other females for protection.

> *Happiness is not a state to arrive at, but a manner of traveling.*
> —Samuel Johnson, eighteenth-century English philosopher

The way that mothers nurture their children, according to Brizendine, "may make babies smarter, healthier, and better able to deal with stress. These are qualities that will carry through their lives and into the lives of their own children."

WHOLE BRAIN FUNCTION

Emotions play a role in decision-making no matter how unemotional you might think you are. Good thinking is emotional in the context of our lives whether we realize it or not. Translation: Human beings think with their whole brain not just one part. Therefore, if, as a mother or in the workplace, you ignore or try to suppress your emotions when making important decisions, you deprive yourself of valuable information and energy. It's that pay-attention-to-your-intuition approach that working mother Dee Dee Myers (along with dozens of other successful women) mentioned in the previous chapter.

When your child care situation requires you to change your work schedule—to work from home, for example, or to work a different shift—if you're guided only by emotion, you might walk into your boss' office and tell him what you need. If your boss says no, you may even get teary, wondering how you will make this work. In contrast, if you think with your whole brain, you'll put together an explanation of how this new work schedule will benefit, or at least be neutral, for the company. You'll pitch the plan to your boss as a win-win—you get what you need and the company does well, too. If your boss says no, you have a basis on which to discuss the situation with your boss or your boss' boss to try to get to yes.

Self-Coaching Break: Whole-Brain Function

Think of something that makes you smile—perhaps your son or daughter bringing you the first dandelion of spring as a special gift. Then think of something that makes you frown—maybe a boss at work reprimanding you for being late. Hold both those visuals in your mind at the same time. Can you do it? Can you balance joy and fear in your mind?

This really is a trick question because biologically, it's impossible. As human beings we simply can't feel fear and appreciation simultaneously. We can't feel hope or appreciation while experiencing sorrow, guilt, or anger. Science proves that we can't experience positive and negative emotions simultaneously. That's the basic concept of whole-brain function.

THE DECISION-MAKING PROCESS

We don't always bring all the right parts of our brain to bear on the decisions we make, either. For good decisions, we need both the amygdala and the frontal cortex. The amygdala is the emotional center of the brain that stores information from the time we were born and warns us of danger or likely bad outcomes. The frontal cortex is where we do our highest reasoning and our best analysis. When we are under stress, however, the amygdala takes over and doesn't give the cortex a chance to operate. That's why we make our best decisions when we are not under stress.

> *Good thinking is a surprisingly emotional phenomenon.*
> —Cathy Greenberg

For employers, this means it makes good business sense to create a corporate culture based on trust and respect. Your employees will make better, more ethical decisions if they feel safe to make a mistake. At home, as mothers, we also make better decisions when we are not under too much stress.

Let's look more closely at the wiring and circuits involved. Whole-brain function frees us from routine and allows us instead to pursue creativity and innovation. When you make a decision with your whole brain, your frontal lobes coordinate and integrate the activity of the brain and nervous system. As a working mother, the frontal lobe will help you organize the logistics of the carpool, but it also helps you play creative games with your toddler and to make good decisions at work.

When frontal lobes are at optimal performance level, the nervous system is in balance and harmony, and our emotions are positive. That's also an essential part of achieving happiness.

MEMORY, FEELINGS, AND SELF-AWARENESS

The brain and spinal cord together make up our primary system for sensing and responding to our environments. We largely relate to the world through our five core senses—sight, sound, taste, touch, and smell. The senses, in turn, deliver stimuli to the brain via the spinal cord. The spinal cord and the brain, which house the central functions of the nervous system, are constantly under fire to safeguard the body from harm. Through feedback loops, they transfer chemical messages among the brain, heart, and muscles, which result in actions or responses from the body.

Over the course of human evolution, brains have developed thousands of connections with complex feedback loops and safeguards to activate and protect us from real or perceived threats. For example, when your fingers touch something hot, your reaction immediately is to yank your hand back to avoid being burned. The experience stimulates your sense memory, and you store the sensory content of the incident in your mind for future reference. Because you are able to draw on that sense memory, you can make better decisions in the future—in this case, avoid being burned again.

You create emotional memories as a result of decisions and actions you take. But unless you cultivate that emotional intelligence, it can be difficult to relate physiological responses to their associated emotional states. For example, it may be that when you get angry, your stomach feels tight. Unless you are self-aware enough to know that your body responds to anger in that way, you may be missing important clues about your emotional state. Society has taught us to sever the association between decisions and their emotional consequences. We are supposed to "think with our brain and not with our heart."

This separation of emotions from logic (or in psychological terms, dissociation) runs counter to thousands of years of human experience. Our early ancestors relied heavily on their sensory perceptions and limbic systems to survive. When threatened, they responded with an emotion of fear, which stimulated them to take action—to flee, to counterattack, or to take some other action to eliminate or get away from the threat. Similarly, when they encountered opportunities to eat or take secure shelter, they acted in response to the positive emotions associated with those activities. In other words, they relied on the emotional content of their prior experience to make decisions that enhanced their chances of survival.

DATA-DRIVEN DECISIONS

Today, however, the decisions we rely on for our "survival" often are determined by data, analytic methods, and organizational hierarchies.

In a world increasingly driven by knowledge and information, this makes sense to a point. For example, when assessing your prospects for financial survival, you lean less on your emotions and more analyzing changes in your portfolio and market trends.

Nonetheless, we tacitly recognize that in many instances, especially those of great complexity and urgency, good decision making involves dimensions beyond the purely rational. Thus, we hear prominent decision makers in the business world, like former General Electric CEO Jack Welch, attribute much of their success to their ability to make decisions based on their gut instincts or their nose for a deal. What such expressions indicate is that the decision maker's rational analysis of a situation is supported, clarified, and augmented by the emotions that associate themselves with that analysis. Those emotions can, in fact, tilt a decision in one direction or another. All the data may seem to argue in favor of one conclusion, but the decision maker— whether you're CEO of a major corporation or managing your home and family—may reject the conclusion if her or his gut instinct rebels against it. On the other hand, if the decision maker goes ahead and makes a decision despite emotional and physiological signals that urge a different course, she may later regret the move and admit she should have listened to her instincts.

Easier Said Than Done

Even if someone recognizes the value of emotionally intelligent decision making, it's still tough sometimes to get a clear reading on one's personal emotional state, especially under stress. Adding to the problem, the stress often occurs at the very moment an important decision must be made. Fortunately, though, human beings can learn to process information in a way that integrates rational and emotional intelligences even in the face of adversity. Decisions then become based on factual analysis with deeply held values in mind, which are the best kind of decisions. Virtually all of the women we interviewed told us that having children changed their value set and changed their decision making. For example, issues of safety and health (yours and your child's) become paramount. When you are young and single, you might have been willing to take risks. When you become a mother, you become far more risk averse.

Happiness and Success

Scientific researchers, including Lyubomirsky, also have linked happiness and success, and in that order, according to the American Psychological Association, the Washington, D.C.-based industry organization. Previous research on happiness presupposed that happiness *followed* success and accomplishments in life, according to Lyubomirsky, who led the study along with co-authors Laura King, Ph.D., of the University of Missouri, Columbia, and Ed Diener, Ph.D., of the University of Illinois at Urbana-Champaign and The Gallup Organization.

Lyubomirsky says they found that this isn't always true. Positive affect is one attribute among several that can lead to success-oriented behaviors. Other resources, such as intelligence, family, expertise, and physical fitness, can also play a role in people's successes. "Our review provides strong support that happiness, in many cases, leads to successful outcomes, rather than merely following from them," said Lyubomirsky, "and happy individuals are more likely than their less happy peers to have fulfilling marriages and relationships, high incomes, superior work performance, community involvement, robust health and even a long life." In other words, happy people are at their best, so they perform well and succeed.

Happiness and Stress

Stress, like happiness, means different things to different people. Something that stresses one person physically, mentally, or emotionally may not necessarily stress another. But there's no question that too much stress is costly, both personally—as in health, family, and relationships—and in the workplace in terms of billions of dollars a year in lost productivity and related health costs.

Science has shown that excessive stress can cause everything from headaches to ulcers, strokes, high blood pressure, hardening of the arteries (arteriosclerosis), and death. It splits marriages, negatively affects the kids, takes its toll mentally, emotionally, and physically on you, and of course derails happiness. Believe it or not, a stressed executive running late for a meeting can exhibit the same heart rate increases, higher blood pressure, and release of hormones as if she or he were being mugged by a knife-wielding thug! That's the brain and body interacting big time. When stress is prolonged, the body—its heart and hormones overworked—becomes more susceptible to illness and disease.

Happiness and Science

Science has varying definitions of stress. It can be the cognitive, emotional, biophysical, and behavioral reaction to a real or perceived threat. The brain tells the body it's under siege—the stove is hot, using the example above—and the body doesn't question whether there may be a misperception, exaggeration, or distortion, but automatically reacts—orders the hand to pull away from the hot object.

Another way to define stress takes a cognitive approach: Stress is the result when reality differs from expectations.

Whatever the definition, however, no one is at his or her best under extreme stress, no matter what they claim. That goes for whether they experience stress in the workplace or at home, or both.

A Fish Story

Have you ever wondered why salmon die after spawning? Their adrenal glands become hyperactive from the exhaustion of swimming up the river to their spawning grounds. The constant "on" cycle causes the internal control mechanisms to fail and the adrenals keep pumping. The salmon, therefore, die from excess stimulation.

If, however, their adrenal glands are removed immediately after spawning, the salmon live on happily to enjoy retirement in their natal streams.

The Positive Influence

Various research studies indicate that the addition of positive emotions—happiness—actually can create positive physical changes in the body.

In 2005, Dr. Michael Miller of the University of Maryland School of Medicine showed for the first time that laughter is linked to healthy blood vessel function. It appears to cause the inner lining of blood vessels to dilate in response to increased blood flow.[6]

The Power of Music

Listening to joyful music can boost your heart health much the same way that laughter does. That's according to researchers led by Michael Miller, M.D., director of preventive cardiology at the University of Maryland Medical Center and associate professor of medicine at the University of Maryland School of Medicine in Baltimore.

Just as laughter causes tissues in the inner lining of blood vessels to expand to increase blood flow, so does joyful music, says Miller, who also led the 2005 laughter study.

On the other hand, listening to stressful music caused blood vessels in study participants to narrow, the 2008 music study showed. Because everyone has different tastes in music, participants were allowed to select their own music based on their likes and dislikes. "We don't understand why somebody may be drawn to certain classical music. There are no words in that, and yet the rhythm, the melody and harmony, may all play a role in the emotional and cardiovascular response," says Miller.

That physiological impact may also affect the activity of brain chemicals called endorphins. "The active listening to music evokes such raw positive emotions likely in part due to the release of endorphins, part of that mind-heart connection that we yearn to learn so much more about," says Miller.[7]

A study at the University of Pittsburgh found that depressed and angry women are more likely to have arteriosclerosis and make lifestyle choices that lead to the condition. Those high-risk factors include smoking, poor physical fitness, and lower levels of good cholesterol.[8]

Studies led by psychologist Sheldon Cohen, Ph.D., a professor of psychology at Carnegie Mellon University in Pittsburgh, also show that stress and negative emotional responses have an effect on human immune responses. Plain and simple, happiness boosts your immune system and can help ward off the common cold.[9]

Put Happiness on your Playlist

Make happy playlists on your MP3 player, and make a point of listening to at least one of them every day. Choose whatever music makes you feel happy. You may want to create more than one happy playlist—one for upbeat happy, one for mellow happy, and so on.

Positive Psychology

Positive psychology shifts the emphasis to what is right with humans, not what is wrong. It is based on a model of possibilities and flourishing instead of illness and dysfunction. As the words imply, positive psychology places the focus on happiness and on an individual's strengths, not weaknesses. By focusing on what's right with our mental models, our lives, careers, and families, and evaluating our sense of purpose in light of the current situation, we can make great breakthroughs in self-awareness, self-love—recognizing work and motherhood are not in conflict—and being more positive. Being more positive actually improves body, brain, and heart function, which in turn leads to better life enjoyment and fulfillment.

> *Positive emotions are essential to human flourishing.*
> —Barrett Avigdor

Corey Lee M. Keyes, Ph.D., associate professor, Department of Sociology at Emory University in Atlanta, is a proponent of promoting and measuring mental health or flourishing in terms of the positive rather than the negative. He's also the co-author with Jonathan Haidt, of *Flourishing: Positive Psychology and the Life Well-Lived*. Flourishing is the result of people feeling emotional, psychological, and social well-being, Keyes said, which can result from experiencing vigor and vitality, self-determination, continuous self-growth, close relationships, and a purposeful and meaningful life.[10]

Building on Keyes' approach, to flourish is "to live within an optimal range of human functioning, one that connotes goodness, . . . growth, and resilience," according to Barbara L. Fredrickson, University of North Carolina, Chapel Hill, and Marcial F. Losada, Universidade Católica de Brasília. Based on their research, the pair suggests a set of general mathematical principles that may describe the relations between positive affect and human flourishing.[11]

Heart Intelligence and Happiness

Scientific researchers also study the physiological methods the heart uses to communicate with the brain to influence how we act, feel, and perform. Heart intelligence is defined by the Boulder Creek, California-based Institute of HeartMath Research Center (www.heartmath .org), as "the flow of awareness, understanding, and intuition we experience when the mind and emotions are brought into coherent alignment with the heart. It can be activated through self-initiated practice, and the more we pay attention when we sense the heart is speaking to us or guiding us, the greater our ability to access this intelligence and guidance more frequently."

The Institute emphasizes the importance of coherence when it comes to our individual physical, spiritual, emotional, and personal well-being. "Coherence, in relation to any system, including the human body, refers to a logical, orderly, and harmonious connectedness between parts. Borrowing from physics, when we are in a coherent state, virtually no energy is wasted because our systems are performing optimally and there is synchronization between the heart, brain, respiratory system, blood pressure rhythms, heart rate variability patterns, and so on. When we speak of heart-rhythm coherence, we are referring to smooth, ordered heart-rhythm patterns. Among the many benefits of coherence are calm, good energy levels, clear thinking, emotional balance, and proper immune system function," the institute maintains. "Each of us is capable of achieving, maintaining, and increasing our coherence . . . through intentional positive feelings—compassion, caring, love, and other such emotions. In contrast, we can quickly become incoherent when we experience negative attitudes such as anger, fear, and anxiety."

The Institute of HeartMath is among the leading organizations that study these physiological mechanisms involving heart-brain communication.

Negative emotions create dissonance in the heart's rhythm and the automatic nervous system. Disharmony leads to increased stress on the ear and other organs. Once again, happiness is key to your physical, mental, emotional, and maternal health and well-being.

Bottom Lines: Exercises to Try

MAKE DECISIONS WITH YOUR WHOLE BRAIN.

Women are known for their intuition. A more scientific way to define intuition is thinking with your whole brain. Our brain has several parts. The mammalian or limbic part of the brain controls our limbic system—respiration, cardiac activity, and nervous system functions. You know the limbic system by its street name—the gut. The frontal lobes of the brain, also known as the executive brain, are where our highest cognitive functioning occurs. The best decisions are those that are made with the whole brain. That may seem obvious but, often, we ignore our emotions—the signals coming to us from the limbic system, and we make decisions using only part of our brain. This exercise will show you how to listen to your body to decipher the messages coming from your gut, and how to use that input to make good decisions. You'll need a timer, a pen or pencil, and a comfortable chair in a quiet room.

1. Sit in a comfortable position, keeping your hands and legs unfolded and relaxed. Make sure your notepad and pen are close at hand.

2. Set the timer for 3 minutes, then press start.

3. Close your eyes and recall, in as much detail as possible, a workplace situation that triggered a significant, negative emotional reaction. The intent here is to help you recognize negative signals that your body sends you. You may recall an argument with a boss or colleague or perhaps a meeting where your ideas were discredited or ignored. Divide the 3 minutes into three distinct phases. Use the first minute to focus on the emotional experience. Use the second minute to tap into the physiological responses that accompany your emotional experience. Devote the third minute to mentally reviewing and arranging your physiological responses so that you can easily write them down when the three minutes are up.

4. Time's up. List your physiological responses to the memory. One method you can use is to jot down in advance a number of possible responses. Once you've done the emotional recall exercise, check off the physiological changes you experienced. But be sure to leave room for responses you didn't think to list in advance.

   Your checklist might look something like this:

   ◆ Rapid breathing
   ◆ Shallow breathing
   ◆ Rapid heartbeat
   ◆ Muscle tension (note where)
   ◆ Dry mouth
   ◆ Salivation
   ◆ Ringing ears
   ◆ Stomach pressure
   ◆ Butterflies in the stomach or gut

   (continued)

5. Now, repeat the exercise, this time focusing on a positive memory. Think of a happy occasion at work, particularly one in which an action of yours had its desired outcome. Again, list your physiological responses:
   ◆ Relaxation (note which muscles)
   ◆ Feeling of lightness
   ◆ Full
   ◆ Easy respiration
   ◆ Involuntary smiling
   ◆ Surge of energy

6. Now you have a list of variables to remind you of your physiological responses to positive and negative emotional states. Your next step is to think of a decision that you will have to make in the near future.

7. Take a seat, relax, and get comfortable. Use your imagination to visualize what your world will be like after you've taken one of the options available to you. Try to put as many details as possible into the picture.

8. Take 3 minutes to tap into your physiological responses. Write down your impressions, then look at the recall list and compare your responses. Do your responses resemble those associated with the previously recalled positive memory or the negative one? If you register an overwhelmingly positive response, you know that your frontal lobes and limbic system are in harmony with your choice, and you have been thinking with your whole brain. Alternatively, if your responses resemble your uneasy physical reactions to your negative memory, then you know that your gut is telling you to reject this option, however rational it may appear. If your responses are mixed, you are not ready to make this decision and need to gather more data, either factual or emotional.

Chapter 3

How to Put the H.A.P.P.Y. in Happy Working Mother

What happy working moms know is you can have what matters most to you.

—Sherry Brennan, mother, and vice president, sales strategy & development, Fox Cable Networks

To be our best for our kids, family, coworkers, and ourselves, we all need to be H.A.P.P.Y. working mothers:

Healthy: physical and mental health.

Adaptive: high Adaptability Quotient (AQ) and good health make you more adaptive.

Proud: of your family and able to derive joy from them as they are.

Proud: of your work and guilt-free because it's part of who you are.

Young at heart: able to find joy wherever you can.

That's the What-Happy-Working-Mothers-Know model for happiness. From these five traits emerge a set of behaviors with a domino effect that positively inspire us to lead fulfilling joyous lives.

Let's take a closer look at each of the elements of H.A.P.P.Y.

H Is for Healthy: Your Physical and Mental Health

Wellness is your responsibility. You're the CEO of the corporation that is your body, and it's up to you to set the tone, direct the operations, and make the right decisions to boost the bottom line, which is your health.

Mood Food

What you eat affects how you feel because chemicals in the body react in certain ways to specific foods, according to the American Dietetic Association. For example, stress can lead to cravings for carbohydrates because they boost levels of sero-tonin, which has a calming effect.[1]

The Details

A healthy body needs good food, enough sleep, regular exercise, and 10 to 12 minutes of peace and quiet a day.

Self-Coaching Break: Healthy Lifestyle Goals

Take a few minutes to answer a few important questions on what physical and mental health means to you:

- What are my healthy lifestyle goals?
- Do I take good care of my health and wellness?
- How do I feel when I am healthy?
- What would support a healthier lifestyle?
- What can I do to promote my well-being?
- What request do I need to make of others to achieve my goals?
- Can I flex my schedule to match a healthier lifestyle?

Feed Your Brain, Don't Starve Your Body

Eating right is easier if you focus on foods that are good for your brain and your heart. Organizations like the American Heart Association, the American Dietetic Association (www.eatright.org), and the U.S. government, including the Departments of Agriculture and Health and Human Services (www.womenshealth.gov; www.health.gov/dietary guidelines/default.htm), have easy-to-navigate web sites with free tips, tricks, and even recipes for a healthier, happier you. Another good source of free information is My Brain Health from best-selling author Daniel G. Amen, M.D., psychiatrist, brain imaging specialist, assistant clinical professor of psychiatry and human behavior at University of California, Irvine School of Medicine, and author.[2]

Make a commitment to incorporate healthy foods into your diet at least twice a week and build up from there. We're not talking about a diet to lose weight; we're talking about a diet to develop the clear-headed stamina and strong health you need in order to do your best both as a mother and at work.

What you eat, when you eat, and in what amount can affect energy levels. Afternoon lows, for example, can be the result of poor meal timing or food choices, according to the American Dietetic Association. The best way to beat those lows is to space meals three to four hours apart and choose low-fat protein and complex carbohydrates for your meals.

Foods for Heart Health

The American Dietetic Association (www.eatright.org) suggests that regular physical activity, the right food choices, and dealing with stress are important to a healthy heart. The nonprofit group also suggests[3]:

- ◆ Limit foods high in saturated fat, which can increase LDL or bad cholesterol levels.
- ◆ Eat more plant proteins, fish, poultry, and low-fat dairy foods.

(continued)

◆ Cook with moderate amounts of olive or canola oil instead of butter, margarine, or shortening.
◆ Foods for heart health include:
  ■ Beans, peas, and barley.
  ■ Soybeans, other soy-based foods (not soybean oil).
  ■ Fruits and vegetables.
  ■ Salmon, tuna, sardines, and mackerel.
  ■ Red grapes and purple grape juice.
  ■ Nuts like almonds, walnuts, pecans, and hazelnuts.
  ■ Green or black tea.
  ■ Onions, scallions, shallots, garlic, and leeks.

What you eat has a huge impact on brain function as well as heart health, says Dr. Amen. In his book, *Making a Good Brain Great*, (Harmony, 2005), he suggests some practical steps for optimum brain health:

◆ **Drink lots of water:** 84 ounces a day which equals 9½ glasses. (**Tip**: Carry a water bottle within arm's reach in your car, and take a sip every time you stop at a red light.)
◆ **Include good fats in your diet:** Despite the anti-fat hype, your body needs fat to function well. The key is to minimize the bad fats—generally those that come from animals and include dairy products, red meat, and pork. (**Tip:** Read labels and use olive oil instead of butter.)
◆ **Include antioxidants in your diet:** Take a good multivitamin containing 800 mg folate, 50 mg B-6, and 500 to 1,000 mg B-12. (**Tip**: If you have trouble concentrating or have low energy levels, try adding 60 to 120 mg of ginkgo biloba to your supplements every day.)
◆ **Balance your meals with protein, good fats, and carbohydrates:** Our bodies need a balance of all three to stay healthy. (**Tip:** Eat a colorful diet.)

◆ **Enhance your health with brain foods:** Brain foods include wild salmon, chicken, turkey, eggs, tofu, soy products, low-fat dairy, beans, nuts, seeds, berries, oranges, cherries, broccoli, oats, whole wheat, wheat germ, red peppers, spinach, tomatoes, and yams. (**Tip:** Try eating at least one brain food a day.)

◆ **Reduce calories:** Research has shown that people who restrict their calorie intake to less than 1,800 calories per day live longer, healthier lives. (**Tip:** Choose to live longer or be more satisfied.)

◆ **Get enough sleep:** Research has shown that adults need eight hours of sleep each night. (**Tip:** If it's a choice between watching TV, checking your e-mail, or sleeping—opt for sleep.)

◆ **Meditate:** Clearing your mind for a few minutes each day is very calming and re-energizing. Meditating 12 minutes each day is an important part of a healthy brain regime, says Amen. (**Tip:** For simple meditation, get into a comfortable seated position, close your eyes, and focus only on your breathing. Try to clear your mind. Thoughts will fly through your brain; be aware of them, but don't engage them. Quiet your mind with your breathing.)

◆ **Exercise:** Aim for at least 30 minutes of mild to moderate aerobic exercise every day. (**Tip:** Check to see if your cable company offers on-demand exercise classes.)

A final word on exercise: Even if you forget its medical and aesthetic benefits, it reduces stress at work and at home. In our research, we asked the more than 1,000 working mothers what they do to relieve stress, and their overwhelming response was "exercise." No. 2 on the list: "shopping . . . alone."

Exercise doesn't have to take a huge time commitment. For time-strapped working moms, Los Angeles health and fitness trainer Debbie Rocker, also a former professional athlete, bicyclist, and spinning pioneer, has a great solution—her WALKVEST®. Picture a fishing vest with lots of small pockets for two-pound weights. Add them up, and you get results just by walking around the house, pushing a stroller, or doing your grocery shopping. It is great for moms pre- and post-pregnancy who want to lose weight and get in shape fast. (Check out the WALKVEST® by Debbie Rocker at www .walkvest.com.

Patty, a nurse and mother of three, knows the difference between feeling healthy and not. "When the boys were little, I felt so stretched that I stopped doing all the things I like to do to stay in shape. I felt guilty taking an hour to run when I had so little time with the boys as it was. Of course, the result was that I was always exhausted and irritable, so the time I spent with them I was not at my best." After that year, Patty made some changes. She was able to shift her schedule to work later so she had more time with the boys during the day when they were awake. She also reserved at least one hour five days a week to run, bike, or practice yoga. "Now, I feel like myself again. I have more energy and I'm in a better mood. I feel like exercising is an investment I make to be a better mom, wife, and nurse."

Your Emotional Health

Being a working mother requires tons of energy, and that means good emotional health. We get that energy and emotional health in large part from the people around us. Although a special hug from a son or daughter goes a long way toward reenergizing us, the reality is that it takes more than that for our emotional health to thrive at work and at home.

A Mother's Story

Jessica works three full-time jobs. She's a mom, CEO of her family's household, and has a successful career as a writer. She loves it all even though some days she's ready to drop from exhaustion. What's the greatest source of her boundless energy? "My daughter throws her arms around me and says, 'Mommy, get ready for energy,' then she gives me a giant bear hug! That's my happiness."

Harnessing the Energy

The effect those around you have on your emotional health may surprise you. To find out, try an energy audit.

Self-Coaching Break: Energy Audit

Create two columns on a sheet of paper. On the left side, write a plus sign. On the right column, a negative sign.

On the left side, list the people who give you energy. Those are people who, when you spend time with them, you feel better than you did before you spent time with them. They put you in a good mood and make you feel good about yourself and the world. Then, in the right column, list the people who take your energy away. Those are the people who, although you may like or even love them, tend to drain you of energy when you are with them.

Be painfully honest with yourself. This list, after all, is for your eyes only.

In some cases, the same people may appear in both columns, depending on the kind of interaction you have with them. That's okay; list them in both columns with a note explaining why.

The energy audit paints a clear picture of those people in your life who give you energy. Try to spend more time with the people you listed in the positive column. Even spending 15 minutes a day talking with one of them can make a huge difference in your emotional health. As far as those people who drain your energy, consider whether you must interact with them. If they're close to you—a spouse or a business partner—you may be able to change your relationship or the way you communicate to make it less draining. If you can't (or don't choose to) limit your contact with them, try telling them what sorts of interactions drain you. They may be able to change the way they talk with you and that could neutralize the negative energy. If you can identify what is draining about that relationship, you can set boundaries that allow you to continue the relationship without sapping so much of your energy in the process.

A Mother's Story

Claudia, a working mother of two, felt stretched to the breaking point—her unhappiness compounded by a husband who didn't help her.

"Why do you work so hard for a firm that doesn't care about you? Do you really think your coworkers respect you more because you neglect your family?" her husband asked one evening.

Claudia took a deep breath to resist her urge to argue with him. It was unfair of Michael to talk to her that way. She was doing her best to balance raising two small children and working the 60 hours a week her law firm expected.

The harder she tried, it seemed the more critical Michael became. After all, she was the one who dealt with the nanny, attended the parent/teacher conferences, and took time off to take the kids to the doctor. Even though her salary was more than half the family income, her husband made her feel guilty for working. Sure, he worked hard, too, but he always got home earlier in the evening, and it never occurred to him to make dinner or play with the kids. By the time she got home at 7, her husband was in front of the TV with the kids playing on the floor nearby.

Claudia felt isolated and miserable. Every waking minute was divided between work and the kids. She had no time for herself, and even less for the two of them as a couple. Claudia felt she was failing as a lawyer and as a mother.

One evening, as she was packing to go on a business trip the next day, all the tension came to a head. "Why don't you just stay away?" Michael asked her. "You're never here anyway, so go work 24 hours a day like you want to."

"That's not what I want!" Claudia shouted. "I'm trying to make this all work, and I don't feel like you're helping!" The baby's crying interrupted them, and brought an abrupt end to the argument.

Later, both agreed they needed outside help, so they turned to a marriage counselor. The neutral setting enabled both to talk about their unfilled expectations of each other and the pressures they felt as working parents.

Michael learned to understand he was exerting unreasonable pressure on Claudia and that his negative comments were deeply hurtful. Claudia learned that she needed to ask for the help she desperately needed. It was unrealistic, the counselor explained, for her to expect help without asking for it.

Claudia also learned to pay attention to her values and respect what mattered to her as a mother and a career woman. She decided that having more time with her kids was more important than her ambition to become a partner in five years. She still wanted to make partner, but she was comfortable taking a slower path to get there. As a result, she went to her boss and was able to arrange to work closer to home and cut back on her travel. It slowed her career progression, but the trade-off was worth it.

Claudia also recognized that superwoman doesn't exist, and that's okay. She can do the best she can and that's enough. Today, Claudia is a happy mother who enjoys her kids' accomplishments, a contented wife who loves her husband for who he is, and she excels in her career, though she didn't climb the career ladder quite as quickly as she had planned.

The Guilt Factor

Guilt, a force that saps emotional health, runs at epidemic levels among working mothers. It's especially prevalent in societies like the United States, where the perceived norm calls for "good mothers" to stay home to raise their children. That's begun to change slightly and very slowly as more women head back to the workforce, in part due to economics.

Since women began to enter the workforce in earnest in the 1960s, the stories have circulated about how children suffer when their mothers work outside the home. As you'll see in detail in the next chapter, the research—and kids of working mothers—indicate exactly the opposite. Children thrive and are healthy and secure when they live in a loving, stable environment. Whether mom works is irrelevant.

Adding to their guilt, working mothers often face a work environment designed for men with stay-at-home wives. The demands of the workplace frequently conflict with the demands of child care. This is changing, though, as more companies adopt flexible work schedules, and the Family and Medical Leave Act offers many parents the right to take leave to care for family members. Still, many working mothers feel that they must sacrifice their careers for their kids and resign themselves to slow or standstill career progression to meet the needs of their families.

Sofia, 33, always knew that even if she had kids—today she has one and another on the way—she wanted to work and develop herself as a professional. Living in Buenos Aires poses difficulties, she says, because Latin American society expects mothers to stay home with the kids. "When I travel for work, my mother and mother-in-law make comments. They're from another generation, though, and just don't understand what it is to be a working mom. Work develops me intellectually and personally, and when I'm home I give quality time to my son."

If you feel twinges of working-mother guilt creeping in, ask yourself what you've contributed this week as a:

◆ Mother.
◆ Working person.
◆ Wife or significant other in a relationship.
◆ Homemaker.

Remember that small contributions can have a big impact over time. If you helped your child learn something new or made her laugh, that's a contribution. If you helped a colleague at work accomplish something, that's a contribution.

A Is for Adaptive

Every working mom knows that change is part of life. Work schedules change; babysitters move away; kids get sick. Just when you think everything is under control, it changes. How we deal with change makes the difference between being stressed and being happy. We call the ability to cope with change your AQ or Adaptability Quotient.

A clear sense of what is important to you and the purpose of your life helps to make change less stressful and easier to navigate. As you learn to adapt readily to more new situations, your AQ increases, too. A higher AQ allows you to become more secure and happier. Whatever your AQ, you can increase it by the decisions you make every day to focus on what is truly important to you.

Adapting doesn't mean giving to others until there's nothing left for you. A popular children's book that you may have read is *The Giving Tree*, by acclaimed poet and author Shel Silverstein. It's the story of a little boy and a special tree that gives up everything for the boy it loves until all that's left of the tree is its stump.

Society tells us that as mothers we are supposed to be like that tree. We are supposed to give to our children selflessly out of boundless love to the exclusion of our own well-being and happiness. Fathers are not expected to forfeit or defer their happiness—society demands that only of mothers. But such an expectation is unhealthy for mothers and for children. Mothers who forgo their own happiness are more likely to live vicariously through their kids. They may even get so involved in their children's lives that they inadvertently get in the way of their children learning to develop their own coping skills.

As mothers, we have unconditional love for our children. We, like the tree, would go a long way to make our children happy and successful. But we owe it to ourselves, our kids, and our work to take care of ourselves as well. To be your best, your most energetic and most joyful self, you need to be able to pursue your own life in addition to your life as a mom. For many women, going to work helps them preserve their sense of who they are as adults, as individuals, and keeps them connected to the real world beyond play dates and storybooks.

For some mothers, staying at home to raise the kids is the fulfillment of a dream, of their life's purpose. We applaud and encourage them to follow their dreams. The point, though, is that mothers are more than just mothers. They also are adult women with their own identities, sense of purpose, and vision for their lives. Happiness comes in part from pursuing the life you believe you were meant to live, and not one that society or family pressures impose on you.

As a working mother, the goal is to create the right boundaries for your children, your relationships, and your work so that you still have something left for yourself. That's a high AQ.

A Mother's Tale

Addie Mae is one of those rare women who combined a lifetime of work with motherhood while never losing sight of what was truly important; she loves life and it shows. She is the happy, retired, working mother of 6 children who live in Texas, Ohio, Kentucky, and Arizona; a grandmother of 26; great-grandmother of 38, and great-great grandmother of 3. Co-author Cathy Greenberg met her on a plane flight. This is her story:

Addie Mae was originally from Louisville, Kentucky, and grew up during the Great Depression. Her father left the family when she was only 2 years old. She started work at age 12, babysitting for the working mothers in her hometown. At age 15, she followed in her mother's footsteps and worked as a housekeeper after school. Her beloved mother had been a housekeeper for the family of Helen Keller.

Addie Mae always looked at life with a view to what could be, and her optimism, hope, pride, and joy shine through her. She went to work in a rubber plant in Alabama, originally as a cook. After 21 years of service as an hourly wage earner, a supervisor, and finally as a member of management, she retired.

At age 58, Addie Mae went to college at Florence State University and loved every minute of it. She always loved learning. (She had been valedictorian of her high school graduating class in 1947.)

The day I met Addie Mae she was returning from her sister Evelyn's funeral. But you wouldn't know it. Her vivacious attitude and sense of abundance as she shared her story radiated from her. She talked about her home, where she loves to serve others her favorite secret recipes for homemade pecan pie, sweet potato pie, and her special Thanksgiving oyster dressing with corn bread.

Her best friend, Sheila, 71, helps brighten her days as does the life she has with her many other friends in Green Valley, Arizona.

Addie Mae's strategy for raising a successful family as a working mother on her own for many years was tough love and instilling an appreciation for service to others. "Serving others is a privilege in life, and I try to do something good for someone every day," she says. When asked about hardships she may have endured, she smiles and says, "Life is what you make of it."

Addie Mae has made a terrific life for herself and all her children. When she gets off the plane, one of her sons is waiting for her. He takes her small handheld case, and she is home. The love and admiration in his eyes are a well-earned reward for a mother who worked, educated herself, her family, and her friends as well as her clients and customers along the way.

Her words echo in my mind all the time: "I try to do something good for someone every day." I like that. As a working mother I wish everyone had that motto. It would make life so much easier for all of us. As my Dad would say, "Try to do an act of senseless kindness as often as possible." To this day, I put coins in expired meters!

—Cathy Greenberg

PP as in Proud of Your Work/Proud of Being a Mother

We don't expect our friends or coworkers to be perfect, but many of us demand perfection of ourselves. (If we're really honest, we wish for perfection in our children, too.)

When we set the bar so impossibly high, disappointment is inevitable. But happiness requires that we take pride in what we have. Pride can come from a job well done, not necessarily a perfect job. If you bring your best to your work each day, be proud; if your child is not the best athlete or the brightest student in school but is kind and considerate, be proud. Pride is a form of appreciation. It is feeling good about what you contribute both in the workplace and as a mother.

If your work is aligned to your values, it's easier to feel proud of it. First, though, you need to be clear about those values. (Try our values assessment exercise on page 9.) Just as you would not take credit for every good thing your company or school does, neither should you take the blame for things you don't like and can't control. Take pride in the contributions you make—personally, directly. Both at work and as a mother, you don't control every outcome, so you can't take credit or blame for them all.

Understanding Your Personal Values

Values are the root of our security, our emotional thermostat. They establish our inner core for decision making, prioritizing, and acting on issues of importance in our lives. Since time, energy, and money are limited resources, working mothers have to make decisions every day on how to spend those resources. If those decisions are consistent with our values, we are at peace with them. If they are not consistent with our values, we feel torn and guilty. Guilt can lead to stress, and stress can eventually undermine our effectiveness and success, both at home and at work.

Think of Claudia, above. Until she and her husband sought the outside help of a counselor, Claudia was wracked by guilt and constantly trying to deal with the work-vs.-home conflict. It wasn't until she clarified her values as a mother and a career woman that she was able to consciously decide to slow down her career progression to make more time at home. She then approached her boss with her decision and was able to tailor a schedule that worked for them both. Then her level of happiness skyrocketed.

Too often we as mothers do a good job but don't feel good about ourselves because we haven't met the high standards we've set for ourselves. Remember, too, that Super Mom—just like Barbie and Wonder Woman—doesn't exist. A good job is not always a job done perfectly. We may place too high a value on the ideal outcome and forget to congratulate ourselves on the capacity, capability, or competence to get the job done at all! It's okay if the dishes end up in the sink overnight or if your children go to school in a less-than-coordinated ensemble. It's also okay if you don't win employee of the month, but you get the job done well and with integrity. Treat yourself as you would your best friend—with kindness, forgiveness, and generosity. Acknowledge your contributions, really appreciate your investment in the result, and you'll be happier with the outcome.

Motherhood Is Not a Competitive Sport

We all hope to raise happy children who are confident, loving, and respectful. That's a big part of what being a successful mother is all about. Sometimes in today's competitive world, though, we lose sight of those priorities. Raising a family becomes a competitive sport. Who walks first; who gets into the gifted program at school; whose child is the basketball, karate, or football star; whose is the most popular; in the most activities; speaks the most languages. Your kids may end up unhappy and resentful, participating in activities they don't enjoy. (Perhaps that's a familiar feeling in your own life.) When it comes to your kids, as with your own life, focus on blocking out the noise emanating from those who view motherhood as a competition.

Instead, focus on and take pride in the beauty in your child and what he or she does. That will set up an entirely different set of priorities. Your kids will get involved in sports or music or other activities because they enjoy them, not because they feel they must do them. Their success at school will be defined as doing their best—whatever grade that turns out to be. You may still need to push your kids to work a little harder or to read more and play less on the Xbox, but you are teaching them to be who they are—not to be someone else.

Y as in Young at Heart

To be young at heart is to be joyful and free of the shackles of negativity that weigh us down and makes us sad. No matter your age, you can be young at heart by replacing negative thoughts with positive ones.

The Institute of HeartMath, mentioned in the previous chapter, has proven that people can improve their health by consciously focusing their thoughts on love and appreciation. After nearly 20 years of research, they've shown that when a person experiences feelings of compassion, love, and caring, his or her heart beats in a smooth, coherent pattern. When that occurs, the body produces more DHEA, the hormone that prevents aging and gives us feelings of youthful vitality. In contrast, when someone is angry or stressed, the heartbeat is a jagged, incoherent pattern. The body produces higher levels of the stress hormone cortisol, which has been associated with diabetes, depression, fatigue, and many chronic diseases.

It's naïve to think bad things don't happen. Of course they do. It's not possible to be happy every moment of the day. To be young at heart is to choose the positive path whenever possible, to be optimistic, and to expect good rather than bad things to happen. It also is to forgive. Holding a grudge creates tremendous negative energy in your body and hurts you in the process. Holding a grudge is like taking poison and expecting the other person will get sick. Let the anger go and move on. Appreciate those you love and those who give you support and comfort.

Self-Coaching Break: Forgiveness and Forgivable Acts

Bad things happen everyday. People may insult, disappoint, or hurt you. You can't control other people's bad behavior. You can, however, control your response to it.

You can choose to be angry and hold a grudge, or you can choose the positive approach. If it's important and you can change it, then act on it. If not, let it go.

Holding on to anger and resentment saps valuable energy that you could use for more positive things like appreciation, learning, or healing. The biological responses to anger and stress are well-documented, while the physical act of forgiveness is still under examination. We do know, though, that the emotional act of forgiveness can speed recovery of one's spiritual well-being, which impacts physical health as well.

TAKE A FEW MINUTES TO ANSWER THE FOLLOWING QUESTIONS AND THINK ABOUT YOUR ANSWERS.

Action

Imagine that you said something cruel to a friend in the heat of an argument. How would you feel when you realized you deeply hurt your friend? What steps would you be willing to take to repair that relationship? How would you feel about yourself and about the person you hurt?

Reaction

Imagine your friend stays angry for a few days and then forgives you. How would you feel when you were forgiven?

Review

How would you show your forgiveness? How would you recognize forgiveness? How would others recognize forgiveness?

Action

Imagine that someone intentionally or thoughtlessly hurts you. For example, a colleague at work spreads a rumor about you that damages your reputation with your other coworkers. Would you feel angry or hurt? Focus on that anger. How do you feel when you think about it? Is your heart racing? Do you feel your blood pressure rising?

Now, forgive that person. Let go of all the anger, even if just for a few moments. Picture it melting like a snowball. Take deep breaths as you let go of the resentment. You may still be right and

(continued)

he or she may still be wrong, but you are making the choice to forgive.

Review

How do you feel now that you have let go of the anger? Is your heart beating more slowly? Do you feel lighter and more relaxed? Does forgiveness feel better to you than anger and resentment?

Insight

If you make a conscious effort to forgive, you will improve your health, your happiness, and all of your relationships, both as a mother and a person at work or at home.

Express appreciation every day. It can be a simple thank-you to another, a note, a hug. It doesn't take much extra effort, but it's good for you!

To be young at heart is to find joy in the simple things of life. Luxury vacations are nice but you can't save your joy for two weeks out of the year. Find joy every day in the rich aroma of your first cup of coffee; in the sweet smell of your daughter's hair as you kiss her goodnight; in the bedtime story you read to your son. Joy lurks in every mundane detail of life; you only need to recognize it.

Happiness Tip: Learn to forgive yourself and others.

Bottom Lines: Exercises to Try

CREATE A H.A.P.P.Y. MONTH
Put happiness on your to-do list, literally. On your calendar begin to set aside time to do the things that will help you to

feel happier. Here are a few ideas, although you know best what makes you happy:

- ◆ Sign up for an exercise or yoga class, and then attend the class, consistently.
- ◆ Make dates to go for walks with a friend.
- ◆ Take 15 minutes a day to practice meditation. If time is an issue, try 5 minutes in the morning before you get out of bed, 5 minutes at lunch time, and 5 minutes in the evening.
- ◆ Set aside time to focus on forgiving someone who has hurt you.
- ◆ Make a values list.
- ◆ Schedule time to talk with someone who gives you energy.

RELAXATION TECHNIQUES

Learning to relax is important for working mothers. That relaxation doesn't have to be expensive or take a lot of time but it can make a world of difference in your ability to happily and comfortably cope. A few options include:

- ◆ Quiet Time
  - ■ Use car rides on your way to or from work as quiet time
  - ■ Use noise-reducing earphones at home.
  - ■ Listen to nature sounds, happy music, or soothing music on an iPod or other MP3 player.
- ◆ Reading Time
  - ■ Take a trip to the library.
  - ■ Visit a bookstore.
  - ■ Take a book and have a cup of coffee or tea at the neighborhood coffee house.
  - ■ Join a book club—or, create a book club of your own.

(continued)

- ◆ Movies
  - ■ Make a list of movies that make you feel happy. Exchange your list with friends.
- ◆ Music
  - ■ Find music that makes you feel good and put it on your MP3 player.
  - ■ When you walk or work out or even when you sit in the break room at work, listen to that music and let it lift your mood.
- ◆ Theater
  - ■ Take in a theatrical production or other cultural event you enjoy. That may include the play at your child's school or local community theater.
- ◆ Sports/Exercise
  - ■ Yoga
  - ■ Pilates
  - ■ Boxing
  - ■ Get a work-out buddy
  - ■ Spinning classes
  - ■ Relaxation classes
  - ■ Stretching
  - ■ Walking, which can be done virtually anywhere, anytime.
- ◆ Drinks or dinner with a friend.
- ◆ Retail therapy/shopping—alone, with family, or friends.

MANY VOICES

If we agree that 50 percent of our happiness is determined by set point and 50 percent is within our control, this tool will show you how to coach yourself to make choices that will lead to your own happiness. Making good choices becomes increasingly important when current conditions (C) are difficult. Self-coaching is a great way to be happier if we can make the right choices for ourselves.

Beginning as very young children we hear many different voices around us. Some of these voices may be positive, some not so positive. For example, our mothers telling us how cute we are or how great we are constitute positive voices. But our siblings telling us they are older and we need to listen to them or obey them may be negative. Our own voices of self-doubt also follow us along the way. These are voices saying things like, can I really do this? Am I smart enough?

One of the voices we hear is society telling us to find happiness in marriage and motherhood. Starting with the women's movement, the voices told us we can have it all. Remember the commercial that told us we could bring home the bacon and fry it up in a pan, and then there was something about pleasing a man?

Our goal is to really listen to those voices that we hear and to understand which ones truly influence our opportunities for success and which ones get in the way of our success.

As your own self-coach, you need to understand which voices play in your head.

You also need to understand which voices contribute to your happiness and which get in the way of your true happiness.

This exercise will help you silence the voices that get in the way of your happiness.

Write down next to each voice if they are enabling positive (E) or disabling negative (D). This will help you identify which voices create which outcome for you when you hear them.

	D	**E**
Mother	_____	_____
Father	_____	_____

(*continued*)

Stepparents	_____	_____
Grandparents	_____	_____
Siblings	_____	_____
Friends	_____	_____
Teachers	_____	_____
Mentors	_____	_____
Coaches	_____	_____
Advisors	_____	_____
Other (TV, movies, society)	_____	_____

Once you can identify the impact these voices, ask yourself the following questions about each of the voices:

◆ Should you listen to them?

◆ When or under what circumstances do they matter?

◆ What does it take to eliminate the voices that no longer provide value, and how do you keep and apply those voices that truly support your strengths and your true desire for success and well-being?

Once these details are understood—you can begin to create a whole new set of internal coaches to complement your motivations for personal success.

Creating new voices and internal coaches.

Knowing that you can choose which voices to keep and rely on, as well as develop your internal coaches, is a true gift.

Here are five steps to building a better group of internal coaches through voices you already know and possibly trust:

1. Write down a new list of voices that evoke positive emotion for you. These internal coaching voices may come to you when you are making decisions, trying new things, or planning daily activities or goals. They may be telling you important details about personal health, child care, or career and personal decisions.

2. Create a new list below by thinking about more recent events or relationships:

	D	E
Spouse or significant other	___	___
Business partner	___	___
Coworkers	___	___
Friends	___	___
Care givers/babysitters	___	___
Support personnel	___	___
Doctors	___	___
Associates	___	___
Instructors	___	___
TV	___	___
Mentors	___	___
Coaches	___	___
Magazines	___	___
Other	___	___

3. Take the time to reflect on their words and how they impact you, your emotions, and your ability to be successful.

4. Next to each of these new potential coaches, write down whether their voices are enabling or disabling influences in your life.

5. Take inventory of those voices with the most positive impact on you. Recognize that these are the internal voices you should be listening to—while those who do not impact you in a positive way should be carefully evaluated.

Recognizing that you have the choice to spend more or less time with these internal coaches and to actually invest in their voices is the first step. Making the choice is the second.

Chapter 4

Guilt—What Is It Good For?

*Motherhood is just as valuable leadership training as
working at Goldman Sachs.*

—Dee Dee Myers, press secretary for former President
Bill Clinton, author

Guilt is the enemy of happiness, and working mothers have their
share of guilt. At work, mom feels guilty she's not spending time
with her family. At home, the guilt centers on not being at work.
Guilt undermines and stymies true happiness for many working
mothers:

- I feel guilty leaving my child at day care.
- I feel guilty when I leave work to pick up my sick child.
- I feel guilty when I ask my spouse or partner to do it for me . . .
  what ever *it* is.
- I feel guilty when I take a personal day to care for my own
  needs.
- I feel guilty when I take a sick day that I should be saving for
  when my child is sick.
- I feel guilty when I don't live up to the standards of my peers
  (mothers or executives).
- I feel guilty when I don't make time for my husband or partner.
- I feel guilty about personal time—even when it's on my
  schedule.
- I feel guilty all the time!

If the guilt doesn't come from within, society will provide it. Despite our many technological advances, U.S. social mores haven't moved far beyond the traditional view of "mom stays at home with the kids full-time while dad works." Those societal expectations send working moms down a long, guilt-ridden road that can fork in very different directions. Some mothers may opt to step out of the workforce; others may forgo or defer their ambitions in order to seek different career paths that allow more time at home, and still others keep going despite the conflicts.

Yaarit Silverstone, a longtime working mother, recalls the pressure she felt when her eldest daughter—now 15—was young. Yaarit's job required her to travel a great deal. One day, when she was picking her daughter up from school, one of her daughter's teachers said to her, "Your daughter is so well-balanced *despite* you, because real mothers put their children to bed every night!" Devastated by that comment and others equally as critical, Silverstone thought about taking a job at a local company so she wouldn't have to travel as much. She found a local job but didn't take it. The thought of doing a job that would not excite and challenge her sufficiently would, she realized, make her unhappy—and she knew that her happiness was important to her family and her work. So she stayed in the position that gave her professional satisfaction, even though she had to travel more than she wanted to at the time. Today she's the managing director for Organizational Effectiveness at Accenture, and is a happy working mother.

As one African-American executive who crashed through the racial and gender ceiling in the workplace says: "The one thing I wish somebody had told me was that it's okay to be a working mom. Conquering my guilt, while having a career and family, has been a lifelong journey."

Happiness Tip: Happiness comes from a full, balanced life that includes hard work, time with loved ones and friends, exercise, celebration, and even solitude. Skimp on any of the ingredients and your recipe for happiness falls flat.

To get rid of the guilt once and forever, working moms need to understand, as Silverstone did, that their happiness is important to their family and that doing satisfying work is an important component of their happiness. These women learn to recognize all that's joyous and right and beautiful in their lives, to embrace the abundance mentality we talked about in Chapter 1, and to give themselves credit for all they accomplish each day. Dwell on the joy of your child's accomplishments, your own successes, and your dreams, whatever they are. Let go of the guilt so you can thrive.

Understanding the Culprit

The dictionary defines *guilt* as the recognition of offending someone, of doing something wrong or breaking the law. As a working mother, you're not offending someone else because you've chosen the fulfillment that work gives you or because you're supporting your family. Neither are you breaking a law because you have a job that takes you physically away from your family five days a week. Although we all *know* that, why do working moms nonetheless feel the nagging tug of guilt, seemingly no matter what they do? Alice, 31, a working mother of two, says her pangs of guilt come from unmet expectations, lack of support, stereotyping by family and friends, or social norms and networks.

Ellyn, 45, mother of three, feels guilt, too, especially when she's on a business trip and her youngest tells her, "I miss you, Mommy."

"That tears at my heart," says Ellyn. But her older children and husband are very supportive; they know how work energizes her, and the oldest is even considering the same career someday. "One way I deal with the guilt is to keep a daily journal for the kids that I'll give them when they're older. It also helps me decide what to tell them now about my job and my feelings, and what to tell them later," Ellyn says.

Remember, we all have a choice. The bottom line is that we choose how we divide our time and efforts, and we probably have more control over that choice than we realize.

"We each have a finite amount of energy, time, and resources," says Renee Trudeau, author of *The Mother's Guide to Self-Renewal:*

How to Reclaim, Rejuvenate and Rebalance Your Life (Balanced Living Press, 2008). "Most of us give away and waste our energy every day without even realizing it—through lengthy, unfulfilling, or sometimes unnecessary phone conversations, endless time on e-mail, the Web, or watching TV; tolerating disorganized spaces that cause us to spend hours looking for items; going to social gatherings or volunteer events we don't want to attend but feel we should attend, and on and on. What we often don't realize is that these activities deplete our valuable energy bank," Trudeau says. If you align your time to your values, you will find that you spend less time on things of little value and more on things that matter.

Valerie, mother of three and an engineer, used to volunteer to organize a big fund-raiser every year for her kids' school. She felt it would show other parents and her kids that she was committed to the school. Instead, she found that she spent countless hours working alone or with reluctant parent volunteers while her own kids whined about why she never played with them. "In retrospect," Valerie says, "I am happier with my decision just to attend but not plan the fund-raiser. That gives me more time to play with or do homework with my kids, and that's what they and I really want to do."

The (Monetary) Value of a Mother

From a strictly monetary standpoint, working mothers are worth every penny. Consider the dollar value of everything you do at home. The estimated value, projected as a salary, was just over $122,700 for stay-at-home moms and nearly $76,200 for working moms in 2009, according to Salary.com.[1]

The Going Rate for Working Moms

Figure out your salary as a mom with the help of Salary.com's MOM Salary wizard (http://swz.salary.com/momsalarywizard/htmls/mswl_momcenter.html).

In 2009, a working mom's "overtime" averaged 17 hours per week in addition to her full-time job hours both at work and at home—nearly double two years ago. The Salary.com survey reported working moms put in a more than 92-hour work week, including full-time job, mom hours, and mom overtime. The survey also shows stay-at-home moms with a 96-hour workweek, with an average 56 hours of overtime.

Salary.com has been following moms' compensation since 2000.

"We started by defining what Mom did and what jobs made up her job description. We surveyed all types of moms to determine the most common roles in her job description. We found that Mom works a hybrid job with over 10 different jobs—each with different salaries—that make up her job description. The job titles that best matched a mom's definition of her work in both the United States and Canada are (in order of hours spent per week) housekeeper, day-care center teacher, cook, laundry machine operator, computer operator, psychologist, facilities manager, van driver, chief executive officer, and janitor," Salary.com said in releasing last year's numbers. The difference in salary between a stay-at-home and a working mom relate to the hours spent on the "mom" job. Whether you're the primary breadwinner in your family or not, that "mom" salary doesn't include the money you bring home from your workplace job.

> *Guilt is a waste of energy. I want to align my energy to*
> *my values, and guilt is not on my values list.*
> —Barrett Avigdor

On-the-job leadership training is an asset that mothers acquire, says Dee Dee Myers, author and press secretary for former President Bill Clinton. It was a political asset for Sarah Palin, Republican vice presidential candidate in the 2008 race.

When Nancy Pelosi became the first female speaker of the U.S. House of Representatives, a reporter asked her how she would manage such a big job. "Are you kidding?" she responded. "Being speaker of the House can't be more difficult than raising five children."

In her book, *Mom-in-Chief: How Wisdom from the Workplace Can Save Your Family from Chaos* (John Wiley & Sons, 2009), author Jamie

Woolf describes mothers as "transformational leaders" because they guide others to reach their highest aspirations.

No wonder so many working mothers we interviewed tell us their job as a mother makes them better at what they do in the workplace—from being more efficient to being better listeners and open to more perspectives. *More than 95 percent of those working mothers also say they're better mothers than they would be if they had stayed at home full time.* The most common reason for that, mothers tell us, is the fulfillment work brings them.

Alice, an elementary schoolteacher and mother of two, says it best. "I absolutely love being a mom, but I work because it makes me a better mom."

It Comes from Within

As working mothers, we perpetuate our own guilt by feeling that we somehow are letting down our children, our partners, and our colleagues at work. Because we divide our time between work and family, we feel that we are somehow cheating both. When we learn to let go of that useless and often debilitating feeling of inadequacy, we can embrace a feeling of peace and contentment in our lives. The prize is boundless energy to invest in doing things we love. We then can do our best as mothers and build on that success to improve our performance in our jobs, too—and vice versa.

> *It's hard to feel bad about yourself when life is good to you.*
>
> —Benita Fitzgerald Mosley, first African-American woman to win a gold medal in the 1984 Olympic Games and CEO of Women in Cable Telecommunications

Most working mothers we talked with would truly love more time with their kids, more flexible working hours, and more time for themselves and their relationships with others. Even if these aspirations are fulfilled, they won't bring true happiness unless you first let go of the guilt. You *can* do it; it's achievable and incredibly liberating for your mind, heart, body, and soul.

A Mother's Story

Mothers derive many different benefits from their work. Here is a sample of just a few from some of the mothers we talked with:

- ◆ Alice, mother of three: "Work helps me focus on making my time with the kids more important. The resentment from before I worked is gone."
- ◆ Tricia, mother of three, including two step kids: "Being a mom gives you a set of connectors to relate with others."
- ◆ Gina, divorced, mother of two: "You learn to delegate without guilt."
- ◆ Mel, single mom, one child: "If you stay at home, you lose the rhythm of life."
- ◆ Maria, mother of two: "I've learned the need to explain clearly my expectations. I've also learned patience and to be more sensitive to others' capabilities and limitations. Everyone is different."

To start letting go of the guilt, first reevaluate what it is you can achieve in a day both at work and at home. Be reasonable in your expectations and take care to put the most important things first. If taking care of clients is the most important thing you do, prioritize it accordingly. If spending time with your kids after work and getting some exercise are both important, maybe you can opt for a bike ride with the kids after work. By prioritizing according to your values, it's possible you won't get to do everything on your to-do list. If you put doing homework with your kids at the top of your list, you may not have time to cook as elaborate a dinner as you would like. If customer service is your number one priority at work, you may not have as much time to mentor younger people on your team. But, when you align your own expectations to your values, not to the values of others, you feel more in sync and less stressed. That's a truism for working mothers everywhere.

June, age 70, guiltlessly gave up cooking, cleaning, and driving to declare an end to her "working motherhood."

Let go of the guilt, say working mothers in a focus group in Buenos Aires, Argentina. Enjoy your work and your kids, and tell your husband or partner that he should be proud of you as a working mother!

Remember Claudia from Chapter 3? She was miserable at home and at work, and her marriage was falling apart until she learned to accept herself, ask for help, reprioritize her ambitions, and take more control over her time. She let go of the guilt and embraced her values as a mom and a career woman. She realized that she needed to take a longer path to partner in the firm in order to spend more time with her family and to relieve some of the pressure created by her business travel. She chose to become a happy working mother even though that meant readjusting her professional expectations for herself.

> *Our goal as parents is to capture the full potential of our kids. At work, we seek to capture the full potential of our employees.*
>
> —Jamie Woolf, author of *Mom-in-Chief: How Wisdom from the Workplace Can Save Your Family from Chaos*
> (John Wiley & Sons, 2009)

A Matter of Priorities

When Claudia recognized that her values and her priorities matter, she realized that living them leads to true happiness. She made compromises, but feels good about them because they are consistent with her values. She realized, as all working mothers must realize, that guilt is good for absolutely nothing but perpetuating unhappiness.

So forget the guilt—there's nothing to be guilty about—forgive yourself, and embrace the joy that is your family, your work, and your life.

A Mother's Story

Christiane Amanpour, New York-based chief international correspondent for CNN, is a working mother and has reported on many of the major crises and conflicts around the world. On May 5, 2007, she spoke at the Simmons School of Management Leadership Conference in Boston about her career and the impact the birth of her child had on her travel into high-risk areas. Amanpour recognized that delivering on her sense of purpose at home and at work was vital to her happiness as a mother and a reporter. She made the conscious choice to do both.

Going into active war zones to report a story is just part of Amanpour's being. As a woman born in the Middle East, she has strong convictions on the subjects of freedom and human rights. After she married, both she and her husband remained true to their commitment to honest and open reporting and communication in the press and to reporting on the plight of others struggling to be free.

After her child was born, she had second thoughts about the risks she was taking in traveling to war zones and into countries and places of unrest. Yet, it was her strong conviction, and her husband's as well, that her work (her sense of purpose) was critical to her happiness as both a mother and a reporter. She always knew her work was a critical element of who she was and that she would have to find a way to fit being a mother into that world.

Her husband has played an important role in supporting her work and their family.

Your Priorities

Now it's your turn. Start by looking at your own priorities in life. Let go of the "overwhelmed-ism" for a moment, and think about a point in your life when you felt you were in control of your time. What were your expectations of yourself and your life? Did you meet those expectations? If so, how did you feel about yourself? How was your self-esteem? If you didn't meet those expectations, why not? Were they realistic and aligned to what you truly value in life?

Self-Coaching Break: Life Matters

To help determine your true values, take a few minutes to think about the following questions, and be painfully honest in your answers:

- ◆ How do you value money?
  - ■ What purpose(s) does it serve for you?
- ◆ How do you value the people in your life?
  - ■ Who is important to you and why?
- ◆ How do you value things in your life?
  - ■ Which possessions mean the most to you and why?
- ◆ How do you apply what you have?
- ◆ To what extent do you compare yourself to others?

Now ask yourself what you truly value in life as a mother, a woman in the workplace, and as a person, and then rank those values in order of importance. At one time in your life, perhaps having a perfect home was high on your values list. But now as a working mother, it's more important to make your home a child friendly play place, so you don't mind putting a ping-pong table in the dining room. Or, you could be at the point in your career where rapid progression to the top is important and you and your family are willing to make the sacrifices it will take for you to achieve your goals at work. There is no right or wrong, only the answer that's right for you.

Your list of values ranked by priority is a snapshot of your current situation in perspective. With this awareness in hand, you can begin to understand the root of potential conflicts you may feel about your dual role of working mother.

The next step is to reevaluate your expectations of yourself and of those around you at home and at work. Armed with this new insight, you can begin to reframe and restructure your daily activities to better match your integrated values as a mother and a working person. As you begin to live your true values as a mother and a working woman, your guilt will melt away. In its place you'll make the decisions of a thoughtful, insightful, happy working mother, and that person is you.

Authentically Happy

Anabelle is a highly respected, single mom with two teenage sons, ages 19 (in college) and 15. For the last 15 years, she's worked and raised her boys in Philadelphia. She's also a role model for others.

Sometimes, Anabelle says, she has to manage her own anxiety to make it all work. But early on she considered her values, and then recognized the importance of where she lived and of her work to help make her life as a single mom and that of her children a success.

"I am basically a happy person . . . when the boys were much younger I would save up my sick time for my kids. Then I got divorced and realized there was no amount of sick days I could accumulate to help me. What I had to face was the reality of raising my children on my own.

"My first thought was to look for a house that was close enough for the boys to walk to school. I loved my home and I really did not want to uproot the kids, but I had to find a way to get the boys to school on time without the support of their father or anyone else, for that matter.

"When I found the house that met our needs, I also considered the fact that they would need to get a meal sometimes on their own, and they would probably be in after-school sports, now and in the future. I found a house that was a little farther away than I was comfortable with from my job, but we made it work. And it did.

"The boys had to get themselves up in the morning and they learned that the first bell from the school yard across the street was their alarm clock. They had five minutes to get to their classrooms. While it was a rocky start, they finally got in the rhythm and our lives settled into a livable schedule. (It took some

(continued)

practice and a few phone calls to and from the school.) Everyone was helpful, and we got it right in the end.

"My sons became more responsible as a result of the move, which enabled me to take on a bigger role with more pay and responsibility at work with more than 50 people in our field staff. I had mostly women reporting to me, and they saw me as a role model for the possibilities and hope they all had, especially under different kinds of life stress.

"I was one of the first at my company to have a PC in my home, and I have been a big supporter of putting PCs in the homes of our staff as well. It took some time, but the company has been supportive of all working mothers over time, and we see the benefits personally and professionally every day.

"If we all hadn't been flexible as a family and I hadn't been flexible with my work and my choices this wouldn't be the success story it is today."

"We all have choices," says Fox Cable's Sherry Brennan. "It's up to each of us to make the right choices that get us where we want to be in life."

Your priorities aren't stagnant, either. They change as you grow and change. What mattered most to you at one point may drop down on your list as your children grow older and you do, too.

You always have a choice, agrees author Renee Trudeau. "When you're an active parent with a busy life and children who need a lot of your energy, you need to be mindful about committing to activities that are not on your Top Life Priorities list."

A Mother's Story

Sherry Brennan, vice president of sales strategy and development for Fox Cable Networks, talks about aligning her career choices with her values.

"Being a mom has meant giving up some aspirations—at least for now—as I have not been willing to put in the hours or do the traveling necessary to do bigger jobs. However it hasn't meant giving up meaningful work—not by a long shot!

"To me, it's all about understanding the price of your aspirations and deciding which matter most, then going about achieving those. I wasn't willing to be away from my son for his first year, so I didn't go back to work until he was 15 months old. . . . I'm still not willing to stay late at the office four nights a week, so I have not put myself in the running for jobs that would require that.

"'Fair' and 'unfair' do not enter into my thinking on this. I think that's a loser's game and a waste of time. The fact is that certain jobs require more time and travel than others. No sense fighting that."

Comfortable Ambitions

Ambition is a tricky word—it can bring great satisfaction and fulfillment to you, your family, and those who work with you. Or it can bring only emptiness. Society expects mothers to defer or deny their own ambitions for the good of their children and families. For some women that is the right choice. For others, fulfilling their ambition is so entwined with their happiness that deferral or denial of those ambitions means a postponement of happiness.

The key is to make sure your ambitions are aligned with your values. For Sherry Brennan, that meant taking a slower career track. For Christiane Amanpour, it meant continuing to go where a story takes her. Both these women lead the life of a happy working mother. You can, too.

No matter the job or field we've chosen, we can be proud of our ambitions. The majority of working mothers aren't afraid to succeed. In fact, 62 percent describe themselves as "very ambitious" in the Working Mother Media survey mentioned in Chapter 1, "What Moms Want."

Work is meaningful when . . .

- ◆ It is inspiring.
- ◆ It is inclusive and involving.
- ◆ It provides opportunity to be creative.
- ◆ It requires learning and growing and is challenging.
- ◆ It connects to the "grand plan."
- ◆ It achieves/exceeds its goals.
- ◆ It provides enjoyable social/work interaction.
- ◆ It is motivating.
- ◆ There is a prevalence of trust.
- ◆ There is no fear.

Diana, 51, married and the mother of a teenage boy, never felt guilt as a working mother. In fact, she says her work helps her son see women as equal to men in terms of career and ambition. "He's proud to say his mom is a lawyer and a professor."

Kim Martin says her daughters, now 10 and 13, used to wish she didn't work because many moms in their neighborhood don't work. Martin, who has an MBA, currently is president and general manager of WE tv. Now, she says, her daughters talk about having children and working. They love the red-carpet premieres and other perks their mom's job provides. In fact, her youngest daughter recently paid Kim the ultimate compliment when she told her she wants her job when she grows up.

Get Savvy

"Success" is every working mother's goal. "It takes more than hard work and talent to succeed; it also takes savvy," says international speaker, coach, and commentator Billi Lee, author of *Savvy: Thirty Days to a Different Perspective.* "Savvy is 'the acquired ability to respond and operate successfully in any environment,'" Lee explains on her web site:[2]

In order to achieve a more harmonious balance between home and office, it is necessary to understand the differences between the personal and professional realms. Getting more savvy about the workplace will help you not only succeed easier, but also decrease your frustration with realities of organizational politics enabling you to determine the best strategies and behaviors in either location.

Billi Lee's Seven Savvy Tips for Success

1. **Get Perspective:** It's Just a Job/Game! Sane people recognize that the workplace is ultimately just a game, albeit a serious one. (Is this stuff really important on our deathbeds?) The workplace has goals, obstacles, rules, teams, players, coaches, referees, and ways to influence the referees. Know the rules, study the players, learn the moves, get coached, and practice. You will win some, and you will lose some. Play hard and then go home to what's really important.

2. **Focus:** What's My Goal? What Price Am I Willing to Pay? Setting a goal is the first step to achieve anything, but the secret is to focus, continually choosing one goal to the exclusion of any other. Before you set a goal, seriously check out the price tag. Decide what you want and what you are willing to give up to get it. Alas, there's no free lunch!

3. **Get Savvy:** Get Real. Grow Up. Savvy is the acquired ability to operate successfully in any environment. It is the organizational "street smarts" that allows you to deal with the world the way it is, rather than the way it is supposed to be. Savvy people are flexible, adaptable, capable of reading people and situations, and able to respond effectively—they are truly "response-able."

4. **Barter:** Success Is a Joint Venture. Since you need the cooperation of others to succeed, the ability to influence is paramount. Bartering, the art of making a deal, is also the art of successful influencing. "I'll help you if you help me." Business is the mutually beneficial exchange goods, services, and favors. Employ the Platinum Rule: "Do unto others the way they want to be done unto." And when you benefit from others, reciprocate . . . pay back.

5. **Get Connected:** Develop an Extensive Network of Allies. Do not limit your network to only those people you like. Your

alliance network should provide you with access to resources, information, connections, experience, and counsel. Allies may be temporary or long-term loyal partners. They may even come from the opposition's camp. They are not always people you like, but they are always people you need. Invest the time, money, and effort to get connected.

6. **Be Resilient:** Capitalize on Change. Resiliency is the ability to utilize the ever-changing environment to your advantage. You don't have to like what's happening, but if you can't stop it or change it, use it. Dinosaurs lacked resiliency. So do many people. Insisting that the world around you shouldn't be the way it is will only land you in a tar pit. Look for the opportunity in the change. Because they are so rare, resilient people will always have career security.

7. **Depersonalize:** Don't Take It or Give It Personally. The company is not your family! The workplace is a system designed to accomplish tasks, not to take care of people. (Taking care of human resources is different.) The organization's mission is to make money. So is yours. Always think of yourself as "You, Inc.," in joint venture with your company and your colleagues. Your boss is your customer. Take care of your business. Then go home and be very personal!

(Find out your "SQ," your Savvy Quotient. Take the Savvy Profile at www.billilee.com and explore options on getting more savvy!)

Workplace Realities

All this sounds great—you simply align your values with your life, open your mind to what's positive in your life, and everything else will fall in place. Of course, we all know it's not quite that easy. No matter what anyone says, twenty-first-century reality is that if you don't work for one of the handful of truly family-friendly companies, living your values may take extra effort. And even if your company is family friendly in its policies, coworkers don't always embrace such approaches.

Self-Coaching Break: Facilitating Your Expectations

When outcomes don't match our expectations personally and professionally, we often feel guilt. That guilt may stem from one of several issues that undermine our success:

- **Resources.** Have you planned for alternative scenarios? As a working mother, for example, do you have backup child care, potential transportation for your child to extra-curricular activities, camp, and more? In the workplace, do you have a backup if you suddenly must leave to take care of a sick child?
- **Support systems.** Do you compare yourself to stay-at-home mothers who have more extensive support networks such as an involved partner, family nearby, extended day care, or live-in nannies?
- **Asking for help.** Do you know when you need help, and are you willing to ask for it? Asking for help isn't a weakness or cause to fret or feel guilty. It is reason to recognize how to forget the fears and overcome the second thoughts that can breed guilt and unhappiness.

Author Trudeau has some suggestions for managing your time and energies more effectively:

- Become proficient and comfortable in saying "no." Practice it. Challenge yourself to say it at least once a week to a request not directly aligned to your top priorities.
- Ask for help frequently. Successful, balanced (and happy) people have robust support systems. Start small. The more you ask for and receive help, the easier it becomes.
- Challenge the "shoulds" when they surface in your mind. They are always a red flag that you're about to do something not because you want to, but because you feel pressure (or guilt)

from an outside influence. Pause and ask yourself, "What is my motivation for taking on this new activity?"

◆ Give yourself permission to change your mind at any time!

Self-Perception in the Workplace

We each possess unique talents and abilities both as mothers and in the workplace. We excel and are proud of it. Yet some in the workplace are slow to appreciate our contributions. That sometimes limits us and negates our competitive advantage in the workplace.

Working mom Kimberly Rath, co-founder of Talent Plus, a global human resources consulting firm, applies the science of talent to help companies—and individuals—achieve their very best. "Talent is a natural ability. . . . It's a person's capacity to achieve near-perfect performance. . . . We know when people are cast in the right position for their talent and continuously developed over the long term, they achieve peak performance. The cumulative effect becomes a key driver of sustainable excellence and a competitive advantage," the company says.[3]

Women tend to underassess their own skills in the workplace, says Sally Helgesen, leadership development consultant, coach, and author of several books, including *Thriving 24/7: Six Strategies for Taming the New World of Work* (Free Press, 2007). Men, on the other hand, tended to overassess their skills, says Helgesen, who analyzed multinational data collected by the Washington Quality Group.[4]

Our successes in the workplace add to our personal sense of pride and achievement, and can offer us yet another source of happiness.

Bottom Lines: Exercises to Try

NAME YOUR FEARS

Fear can lead to behaviors that block happiness. However, naming the fear and confronting it can help to eliminate it and get us back on track to finding our happiness.

Try this exercise:

1. Look at the following list of fears and check all that apply to you:
   - Fear of failure.
   - Fear of not being a good mother.
   - Fear of not being good at my work.
   - Fear of not being a good wife.
   - Fear of living in poverty.
   - Fear of not being able to learn new things.
   - Fear of being alone.
   - Fear of being too successful.
   - Fear of being too powerful.
   - Fear of losing control.
   - Fear that if you start crying, you may never stop.
   - Fear of_____.
2. For each fear, ask yourself the following questions:
   - Why am I afraid of this?
   - Has this ever happened to me?
   - If so, how did I survive it?
   - If not, is there a voice in my head that tells me to fear it?
   - Where did that voice come from, and why don't I choose to silence that voice?
   - What is the worst that could happen? How can I survive the worst?
   - If my best friend confessed these fears to me, what would I tell her?
3. Fear can lead to behaviors that block happiness. Finish the following sentence by checking which of the following applies to you.
   I would be a happy working mother if I could:
   - ❑ Be less blunt.
   - ❑ Be more open to input.
   - ❑ Be less impulsive.
   - ❑ Be better at setting my expectations.

(*continued*)

❑ Be more forgiving.
❑ Be less ego-based.
❑ Be less fearful.
❑ Be less judgmental.
❑ Be more inclusive.
❑ Be _____.

4. Now ask yourself why you feel that way and what you could do to change that feeling for each item you checked. For example, if you feel you are too judgmental, ask yourself why. Did others judge you when you were younger? By whose standards are you judging them and why?

Chapter 5

When Mom's Not Happy, No One Is Happy!

Half the battle in life is choosing something you love to do. You need to have that sense of accomplishment in your heart and to serve people the way you would like to be served.

Sharon Allen, mother of two, and assistant chief of police, Tucson, Arizona

Mothers set the tone for their families. More than 95 percent of the women we interviewed agreed that when they're happy, the rest of the family is happy. Yet, many of the same women admit they don't invest enough time in doing the things that make them happy. They're too busy taking care of everyone else at home and at work.

Our research and the research of many others before us shows that the best thing any of us can do for the happiness of our families is to love and accept ourselves and choose happiness every day. Your happiness is not a luxury, it's a necessity, so it should be on your priority list.

As women, we tend to be hard on ourselves. We seek perfection in everything we do. Starting in childhood, we get messages from TV, magazines, and well-meaning teachers and relatives that we should be pretty and sweet, strong and independent. The Barbie doll has evolved from a suburban housewife to a doctor or policewoman, but she still looks a lot closer to perfect than any real women we know. All that perfectionism gets in the way of happiness.

The happiest working moms we met in our research were those who were joyously, unapologetically imperfect. They are the women who know their strengths and build on them, and who work around their weaknesses. Their bodies may not be perfect or their houses may not be tidy but they get the important things right. They love their kids, and their kids feel that love every day. They enjoy their work and derive deep satisfaction from it. They have defined their values and excel in those things that are truly important to them. For everything else, good enough is good enough.

Happiness Tip: Half the battle in life is choosing something you love to do. The other half is celebrating your successes along the way.

"If you are not happy with yourself, you can't be happy," says Danielle, a happy working mother of three in Tucson. "You need to get to a point where you don't care what people think, and you gain confidence."

Authentically Happy

Danielle, a hairdresser, salon owner, and mother of three in Tucson, shares one of her tips for happiness:

"I love to sing, so I think I sing well. My friends tell me I sing horribly, but I don't care.

"When I was in grade school and middle school, kids teased me for being chubby. Now I am a hairdresser and my clients always tell me how great I look. My work helps other women feel confident, too, because they look their best. Confidence comes with age, and confidence is attractive."

Stop Shopping!

Many women become overwhelmed with their desire to be enough. Are we beautiful enough, well-dressed enough, popular enough, giving enough?

To demonstrate that you are enough, you strive to obtain material goods, access to social functions, or status through relationships, male or female. When women get into this trap they often tell themselves that if they have more—more clothes, shoes, handbags, jewelry, friends, boyfriends, lovers, better husbands, or access to more social events—they will be classified as more successful, better people, and ultimately revered.

Why do women do this? Is it really and truly enriching their lives, or who they are or want to be? Are they perhaps, instead, getting back at someone for all the times that person made them feel inadequate? Are they trying to live up to someone else's opinion of who they are or what they should have accomplished in their lifetime?

Wouldn't you rather have something that is truly valuable, instead of collecting objects, invitations, or access to people merely to satisfy the opinions of others?

To test this possibility let's look at the following questions:

1. Which best describes the reasons you are making non-essential purchases?

    Put checkmark next to the statements that you feel best represents your feeling during a purchase. Pick your top three:

    ❑ Satisfying a personal need to buy something.
    ❑ Satisfying a need to demonstrate your ability to make a purchase in front of someone.
    ❑ Satisfying a need to make the salesperson feel successful.
    ❑ Satisfying a need to give yourself a gift.

(continued)

❑ Satisfying a need to provide yourself with a required item for work or play.

❑ Satisfying a need to be the first to have something for status.

❑ Satisfying a need to be prepared for something like an event (a social occasion like a wedding, dinner, date, or meeting).

❑ Satisfying a need to be generous to others (for example: buying a gift item).

2. When you make a decision to actually complete the purchase, do you generally feel the following? (Circle the answer that most frequently represents your emotion):

Excited and delighted with your purchase. YES NO

Guilty and ashamed of your purchase. YES NO

Depressed after the fact (especially at the thought of the bill or invoice when you have completed the purchase). YES NO

Satisfied by the accomplishment of completing the purchase. YES NO

3. After you've taken your purchase home, how often do you return your purchases for a refund or an exchange if the purchase is for yourself (circle the appropriate response)?

Always

Often

Sometimes

Not Often

Never

4. Ask yourself these questions:

◆ In looking at your buying history do you see a pattern that might help you understand why you make purchases?

◆ If you believe you have enough things, the questions to ask yourself are (place checkmark next to each that applies):

❑ Do I really need to make this purchase and what will it do for me after I have it?

❑ Can I be happy without this purchase?

❑ Can I ever really have enough?

❑ Do I really need any more than I have right now?

Often we make purchases to comfort ourselves and to prove to ourselves that we are deserving—deserving of something new, something that will bring us attention and compliments, as well as serve our need to feel loved and successful. Knowing the difference between buying things we want and buying things we need is important to our self-esteem and overall happiness (not to mention our bank accounts). Going without something we dearly want is not the answer. But making a purchase for the sake of overcoming a feeling of not being enough is not the answer either.

We all know in our hearts what is enough. Choosing to indulge ourselves on occasion is fine, if we can afford it. The power comes in the self-awareness that we have the choice and that we are honest about the reason why we make any purchases.

The Happiness Traps

Many of us fall into the "thinking traps" that block our happiness. Those traps lead us down a road that veers away from happiness. Working mothers face twice as many traps as they try to be the perfect worker and the perfect mother. Across all the focus groups we conducted around the globe with entrepreneurs and both salaried and hourly employees, working mothers consistently talked about the same traps. Among the most common:

◆ Supermom
◆ Money Matters
◆ Whose Needs
◆ Resentment
◆ I Am What I Do
◆ Self-Doubt
◆ Setting Your Pace

Let's take a closer look at each of these nemeses.

SUPERMOM

Driven by the fear of not being good enough, working mothers seek perfection both in the workplace and at home without realizing that perfection is unattainable in either place.

The prototype of the ideal mother is the one who is always there to help with homework, read a story, or bake cookies for the class. She's always available, physically and emotionally; never loses her cool; never forgets to sign a permission slip or to bring the oranges to the soccer game. The ideal worker is one who always gets the job done. Whether an executive or a fast-food clerk, she's the one who's there when people need her, who does her work impeccably, who mentors others, who makes customers or clients happy, and who makes her boss look good. She never loses control, never misses a deadline or an appointment, and never makes a mistake.

You don't hold your children or spouse to such a high standard. You love them and accept them as they are. When your children grow up, you don't want them to make themselves crazy in the never-ending pursuit of perfection. You want them to love and accept themselves so they can be happy and at peace. Why not do the same for yourself?

You're not perfect—and that's okay, says Sharon Allen, mother of two and assistant chief of police in Tucson, Arizona. "You need to forgive yourself. Laundry can wait! Accept that you can only do your best, that you're human, and don't give up on yourself. You may take a different path than you thought, but the detours are worth it because you learn more from your failures than from your successes."

A Mother's Story

Always a career woman, Sharon Allen panicked when she had her first child. "I thought, 'How can I have my career and a child?'" recalls the now-longtime law enforcement official. "The minute I held her, I knew she was the most important thing in my life."

Thus began Allen's personal and professional journey as a working mother and wife (she's been married to her husband for 28 years) that blended child care with police work. Whether she was a detective or now the assistant police chief, she had irregular hours and at one time worked a 4–10 shift giving her three days off—one day to take care of the house, one to be at the kids' school, and one for herself. During that time, she earned her BS + Masters Degree in Education at a local college, and even worked part-time as a security guard at a mall to make ends meet.

"I was doing well with my career even as a working mother before it was in style . . . and yes, sometimes I felt I had to work twice as hard. I made mistakes, too, such as when my son was in high school, and I badgered him to cut his long hair. 'Mother,' he said, 'I am a good person . . . I follow your rules and stay out of trouble . . . If I have long hair, it's not a big deal; I learned to compromise. (He's now at West Point!)

"That 'S' on my chest can fade sometimes. I used to crash and burn and sleep on the weekends. People say I am so successful— I say if my children have grown up to be self-sufficient, good citizens, I've been a pretty good mom. Half the battle in life is choosing something you love to do. You need to have that sense of accomplishment in your heart and to serve people the way you would like to be served. That's key."

Money Matters

Throughout all of our research and conversations with working mothers, money stood out as an important motivation for having a job or career. Without a doubt working mothers contribute significantly to their families' income. Of the women we surveyed, approximately 43 percent said they contributed more than 40 percent to the household income. If money is the only compensation a working mother receives, however, she is definitely underpaid. Work demands tremendous time and energy, and takes working mothers away from their loved ones. "Before I had a baby, I was happy to work on any type of assignment," says Stella, 32, a consultant who recently had her first child. "Since I've been back from maternity leave, I feel strongly that the work should be meaningful; otherwise, I'd rather stay home with my baby."

Happy people are those who are able to find joy in their work or find work that gives them joy. That doesn't mean you must necessarily work for world peace. It simply means that you find things you enjoy doing and remind yourself on a regular basis why you enjoy them. Working hard at something you enjoy is far less stressful than simply working hard. Danielle, the hairdresser from Tucson, is a great example. The hardships she endured make her story of happiness even more compelling and her happiness triumphant. Hers is the story of a working mother who chose love and happiness in circumstances that would make many women angry and bitter.

A Mother's Story

Danielle's story is one of love and hardship, strength, and thriving despite impossible odds. When she recounted her story, I was speechless. She is a beautiful woman in her early 30s, with a big smile, great hair, and a fun wardrobe, who is always laughing and hugging her clients. You would think she didn't have a care in the world. Her story made me realize how powerful love and a positive attitude can be, even under the most difficult circumstances.

—Barrett Avigdor

Danielle met Keith on the third day of freshman year in high school. Keith was fun and romantic. Danielle was a chubby girl in high school, and Keith's love and attention boosted her self-esteem and made her feel beautiful. They dated on and off throughout high school and married right after graduation.

Keith went to college and earned an accounting degree. Danielle went to beauty school and started working in salons. When Keith started his first accounting job, he and Danielle started a family. Their first son was born with Tourette's syndrome and attention-deficit/hyperactivity disorder. Tourette's is a neurological disorder that causes tics and twitching and/or sudden outbursts. Two years later their second son was born, and a year after that another son. For seven years, Keith and Danielle had the perfect marriage. They were deeply in love. They had fun with the kids, and they were active in their church. They were doing well financially and building their savings. Their home was full of love and laughter.

One day while working around the house, Keith pulled a muscle in his back. The doctor prescribed the narcotic Vicodin, and that was the beginning of the downward slide. For a long time, Danielle had no idea anything was wrong. Keith went to work every morning and came home every evening. She noticed money leaving the checking account, but she never asked him about it.

By the time she confronted him, Keith was taking 30 pills a day. He was getting the Vicodin from the tenants of their rental properties and taking the drugs instead of cash for rent. He would take valuables from their home and pawn them to get money for drugs. He even pawned the Xbox they had bought for the boys.

Finally, Danielle confronted Keith and insisted he go to a detox program. When he went into the program, she changed the locks on the house. She had three young children at home, and she had no idea whether Keith had given the key to some of his drug addict friends.

(*continued*)

When Keith got out of rehab, he went downhill fast. He moved into one of their rental units and started doing crack. In less than a year, he went from being a respectable accountant with a wife and a family to being a drug addict living on the street. He would come to the house once in a while to ask for food or money, and it broke Danielle's heart to see him in such a state. She always gave him something.

For two years, she did not tell her boys what had happened to their dad. She wanted to preserve their image of him as the great dad he had been. She simply told them that he had to go away. When the kids would notice items missing from the house—furniture, a TV, a camcorder—Danielle would simply say "Daddy needed it more than we did." Then she would add, "We don't need those things. This house is made of love."

In the meantime, Danielle opened a salon with Kathy and Sheri, two of her best friends. She loves her work, which she sees as giving women self-confidence and helping them see how beautiful they are. She loves her business partners, with whom she laughs and cries, and relies on every day. Their support, along with that of her parents and siblings, helped keep her strong and optimistic.

On what would have been their 10th anniversary, Keith was waiting outside the house when she got home from work. He was clean and sober, and he apologized to her for all the hurt he had caused. They reminisced about happier times; he played a while with the kids, and left. Three weeks later, he was hit by a car and killed. He was 35 years old.

Danielle waited two years before she told her oldest son the truth about his father. He listened carefully and nodded. "For a long time, I blamed you for the fact that Dad was gone," he told her. "I'm glad you told me the truth now."

He paused and then looked at his mom again, "So the Xbox and the camcorder, it was Dad . . . ?" Danielle nodded. "That's okay," he said. "We don't need that stuff. This house is made of love."

Postscript: Three years after Keith's death, Danielle remarried. She and her new husband took two honeymoons—one before the wedding with Kathy and Sheri, Danielle's parents, and other friends for a week on the beach—and one after the wedding to take the boys to Disneyland.

Whose Needs?

Females have been caretakers and nurturers for as long as there have been babies. We become fiercely protective of our children—biological or adopted.

Pleasing our children—and others—can be a full-time job if we allow it. That's why it's so important to set boundaries for yourself and those around you. As a working mother balancing the demands of family and a job, you have less time and space within which to draw those boundaries. Your life is a marathon, not a sprint. To win, we must learn to pace ourselves. Make yourself as important as your children, your partner, and your work.

Self-Coaching Break: Ask the Right Questions

Knowing how to ask yourself the right questions can help determine if you're on the right track for your life and your career, and if you're making decisions that are right for you.

- Is this the right thing to do at this time, or ever, in my life?
- How will I know? What will be the measure?
- Is there a better time to do this?
- Is this right for me as a mother?
- Is this right for me as an associate?
- Is this right for my child's overall well-being?
- Will I be happier, healthier, or better in any way if I agree to this?
- Is there a short-term or long-term gain?
- How can I measure my success if I agree to do this?

Remember Sue, the working grandmother mentioned in Chapter 1? She's a caretaker extraordinaire—raising her grandchild; focusing on the well-being of her two children and her husband; taking care of her elderly parents, and devoted to her job. She gives selflessly and in abundance, and derives great joy in doing so. Yet Sue also thinks of herself. She makes time in her busy schedule—one day every week—to nurture herself and her own needs. Sue lives her values at home and at the school where she works, and embraces the essence of true happiness in all she does.

Self-Coaching Break:
<u>Pleasing Others and Pleasing Yourself</u>

Knowing your priorities is a big part of learning to find your happiness. Take a few minutes to think about some of the most stressful things you do in your life, and ask yourself these questions about each one:

- ◆ If I do this for you—how will it make me feel (happy or unhappy)?
- ◆ Do I have time to do this for you or to make this commitment?
- ◆ What needs of mine will be put on hold to make this work for you?
- ◆ Do I please others because I need to be liked—or because I like doing for others?
- ◆ Can I still take care of my needs if I do this for you?
- ◆ Will doing this contribute to my well-being?
- ◆ Am I pleasing you simply to make things easier for me?
- ◆ Is there something I need to do differently to please myself?

Every relationship we have can be defined as an energy flow between us and that person. In a well-balanced relationship, the energy flow goes both ways. You give energy to that person and they give energy to you. Many relationships are more one-sided.

Figure 5.1 Power Map

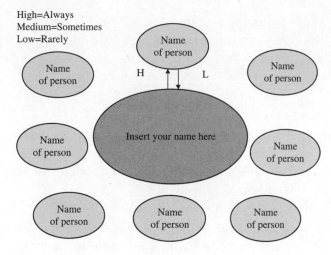

You may be the giver or the receiver of energy, but it doesn't go the other way. Take a look at the Power Map in Figure 5.1.

Who requires your time and energy?

◆ Spouse or significant other
◆ Boss or business partner
◆ Children
◆ Clients or customers

Track the energy flow.

◆ Put your name in the middle oval.
◆ In each of the other ovals, put the name of someone you interact with often.
◆ Draw an arrow pointing toward those people in whom you invest time and energy. Indicate if you investment in

(continued)

them is high, medium, or low in terms of amount of time and energy.

◆ Draw an arrow pointing toward you from each person who gives you time and energy. Those are the people who energize you. Indicate if their investment in you is high, medium, or low.

Check the results.

◆ Look at the arrows.
◆ Where is there an imbalance between what you are giving and what you are receiving?
◆ Why does that imbalance exist?
◆ What can you do to balance that relationship more? Do you need to give less? Demand more in return?

Resentment

When you feel as if you're stretched thin between work and home, it's easy to feel resentment—toward a partner for not helping more at home (or about not having a partner to help at all), toward your boss for not being more understanding, toward those stay-at-home mothers whom you think judge you harshly, and toward your kids whose demands seem endless. Your stress and your fatigue can simmer into an overwhelming silent anger that interferes with your happiness.

One of the most important paths toward finding your happiness is to let go of that anger and learn to forgive. Forgive yourself; forgive your family; forgive your friends; forgive your coworkers; and forgive those you believe pass judgment on you or thwart your dreams. If you let go of the anger—truly let go—you'll feel an immense relief that will allow space in your head and heart for happiness. Hanging on to resentment creates a stone in our hearts and minds that blocks our happiness.

As mothers we strive for the capacity to be loving and forgiving human beings. How we choose to forgive and demonstrate that love for others is a gift we share with and teach our children. Forgiveness is a crucial component of unconditional love. Yet at times we are so deeply and genuinely hurt by the actions of others it seems we will never find the space to forgive.

Whether in your mind and heart you see forgiveness as a moral issue, a religious one, a legal one, or simply as necessary to your physical and emotional health, it permeates the fiber of your very being. Regardless of its roots, forgiveness must be all-embracing if we are to be truly whole and happy. Any limits we impose on our capacity and willingness to forgive are limits imposed on our own happiness. When we withhold our forgiveness, we harm ourselves as well as others.

Forgiveness is an important issue to think about carefully and resolve successfully if we are to be fully healthy, happy adults. The act of forgiveness goes beyond mere kindness or perfunctory words. It offers its own special spiritual, moral, and biological healing to the mind and body. In our imperfect world, there is no shortage of opportunities to show forgiveness. Those are opportunities for growth and self-healing, as well. The seed of forgiveness is in every human being. Everyone is capable of forgiveness. More important, we all are capable of being forgiven. The choice is ours.

Authentically Happy—A Story of Hope

Michael S. Barry, D.Min., author of *A Reason for Hope* (David C. Cook Publishing, 2004), and Director of Pastoral Care at Cancer Treatment Centers of America in Philadelphia, has a formula for forgiveness. It's a mixture of Theophostic healing (from *Theos* = God and *phos* = light) and narrative therapy, or healing through the power of reflection and self-expression, whether singing or writing poetry.

The premise of Theophostic healing comes from the theory that "truth will set you free," Dr. Barry says. "Often, it is a lie we

(*continued*)

tell ourselves or irrational thoughts we are thinking that keep us enmeshed in hatred and unforgiveness. By seeking the truth about ourselves, as well as what happened to us, we are better able to understand the events without shame or blame. By relieving ourselves of the burden of shame or blame, it opens our hearts to the possibility of forgiveness."

It's important to distinguish between forgiveness and a forgivable act. For example, our actions may unintentionally create a misunderstanding or unfulfilled expectations. Those are forgivable acts. It's then up to the person who was the target of our actions to decide whether to forgive. Some actions are both forgivable and worth forgiveness. Intentional acts of harm or cruelty, however, are not forgivable acts, but we nonetheless are capable of forgiving them. Even the most distressing circumstances like war or crime, which are not forgivable acts, can be forgiven. Our capacity for forgiveness is what makes us truly human.

Each of us must decide for ourselves whether to forgive or hang onto the wasted emotions of anger, pain, and resentment that certain acts—forgivable or not—can cause. The biological responses to anger and stress are well-documented. The physical activity of forgiveness is still under scientific examination, but we do know that the emotional act of forgiveness can speed recovery of our spiritual well-being, which many believe deeply affects our physical health as well.

Once you realize the importance of letting go of anger and learning to forgive, practice doing so. Forgiveness is an art that isn't mastered overnight. It will get easier, though, with practice.

One of the first steps in learning to forgive is learning how to rid yourself of resentment. To do that, you must first determine the cause—or causes—of any resentments you carry and then decide what it would take to dissolve them. If you need more support at home or at work, what can you do to get that support? Have you asked for help? Maybe your children are old enough to help out a little more than they do. Maybe your partner could shoulder a little more responsibility.

You also must consider whether you are trying to do more than actually needs to be done. How important are the issues that are creating resentments and blocking your happiness? For instance, does the house really need to be spotless every day? Is it imperative that you work on that report until after midnight? Don't lose sight of the fact perfection is *not* an achievable goal.

The Guilt Checklist

Throughout this book, we talk about guilt and excuses we all use that decrease our effectiveness and our happiness. Take a look at this list and then develop your own list of guilt and excuses. Then make a commitment to try to eliminate them, from your thoughts as well as your actions.

The Guilt and Excuses Checklist
◆ Not learning from our mistakes
◆ Making excuses
◆ Using people
◆ Feeling guilty about X
◆ Setting our sights on Mr. Right
◆ Other_____

A Mother's Story—A Mother's Victory

Jayne Rager de Garcia Valseca, 42, is not your typical working mother. But then, her story and incredible ability to find joy and forgiveness in the depths of despair and hardship aren't typical, either.

Right now, Jayne is being treated for breast cancer at Cancer Treatment Centers of America in Philadelphia. It's not the first time she's had cancer. At age 38 she was diagnosed with breast cancer and made a complete recovery. This time around, though, she's had to learn an extraordinary kind of forgiveness to help her get her life back.

(continued)

"I had a storybook life, and I was sure cancer was a thing of the past for me. Then a horrific thing happened to us. We were living in central Mexico and excited about our impending vacation with the kids.

"My husband and I were returning home after dropping the children off at school and were about three-quarters of a mile from home when we were suddenly ambushed. The armed attackers stopped our car on a side road. They broke the windows and pulled us from our car. It all happened in a matter of seconds, but it was noisy and full of panic.

"My husband was hit over the head with a handgun. They forced us into a get-away car. We were blindfolded with pillow cases over our heads, and our hands and feet were bound with duct tape. After about 15 minutes, they released me into a wooded area on the side of the road. I didn't know what was happening. They took my husband somewhere else, and left me with a ransom note. They wanted a multimillion-dollar ransom for his return.

"What followed was absolute hell. They held him for seven and a half months in a small closet with no windows, bright lights, and loud music day and night. He was naked most of time, barely alive, sleeping on a cold floor, and given very little food. They beat him daily, and shot him at close range twice—once in the leg and once in the arm. They did this to take photos to send me to motivate me to send the ransom—which we didn't have. I didn't know what to do. I simply had to find a way to go on and get through it.

"During this time I despised these people for what they were doing to my husband, and what they were doing to our lives. I was angry and wanted revenge. I had a fantasy of beheading them all like a samurai. These thoughts brought me great pleasure. I spoke with a local minister, who told me to pray for the kidnappers and for peaceful resolve. He gave me a beautiful prayer, but it wasn't enough. Life was a living hell for all of us. But I feel it was hardest for me—I had to keep it all together for the children and for the family. I was afraid to show my real emotions. I couldn't even cry when I wanted to because there would be no turning back: the floodgates would open and I thought I would never recover.

"After my husband was finally released, I was thrilled to have him back with us, but I was overwhelmed by the cruelity of his treatment and his physical condition. He was only 90 pounds by then and could barely walk but was still such an amazing, positive person, with a renewed appreciation for every second of life.

"I was the person it took the biggest toll on in the end. Within weeks of my husband's return, I found a lump in my breast again. When I got the diagnoses, I wasn't even surprised, I had been through so much. I felt numb to the news.

"When I arrived at Cancer Treatment Centers of America, the Director of Pastoral Care, Michael Barry, introduced me to the idea of forgiveness being an act of self-love, and an important tool for inner healing. I knew I didn't want to let all of the hate and anger continue to damage me, but the idea of forgiving these criminals seemed a bit of a stretch. I tried to justify my rage. But Barry came back at me with, 'Look, this is the gift you give to yourself, Jayne.'

"My homework was to write the kidnappers a letter. I wrote five pages telling them everything I thought about them. It felt so GOOD! It truly felt like a pressure cooker when the top blows off.

"Dr. Barry told me to write another letter, but this time try to find empathy for them. He reminded me of how imperfect we all are, and that under the right circumstances we are all capable of doing some pretty rotten things. I sat down to write, but had nothing more to say. I decided to relax, breathe deeply—a kind of meditation—and started to think about these criminals as babies. Then I imagined what they must have gone through in their lives to become the criminals they finally became. It took about an hour, and during this time of meditation. I felt the physical relief in my own body. The places I felt the most relief were where the doctors had found the tumors.

(continued)

"I started to think how much of this was a result of my own toxic retention of negative thoughts and emotions, my own way of processing things (my control). I felt a huge internal shift. Since then, even my therapy was easier to take; I would get up after my treatments and not lie around depressed about them. I took a positive outlook toward my own recovery, and am very active in making it happen. I have a very positive attitude now. I am making a remarkable recovery, and hope others will truly understand the importance of forgiveness and the psychology of positive thinking in your own recovery."

Postscript: As Jayne's recovery continues, she's writing a book about the experience in Mexico—*While Mariachis Played*.

I Am What I Do

Many working mothers feel they are insignificant without their jobs. They mistakenly believe that the prestige of their work or their financial contributions to their families is what gives them value. Of course, their children would immediately tell them that's not true. Rather than realize their intrinsic worth as human beings, these mothers think their worth is contingent on a paycheck or a job description. It's not who they are that counts, they think, but what they do or how much they earn. This kind of thinking can trap you in a job that might give you a fancy title or six-figure income but doesn't bring you joy.

Happiness begins when you learn to accept the fact that you are loved and valued for who you are—not what you do. Happiness begins when we learn to love ourselves. Regardless of your choice—to stay at home as the CEO of your family, or stay in the workforce—it's important to know you're loved and appreciated for the value you add as a happy person. In truth, we can all be happy working mothers. After all, we work at home just as hard—if not harder—than a fully employed associate. We all have a job in life—at home or at work. Our success in either role is measured by our relationships—not our titles. We are successful because of the company we keep, not the money we make.

A Mother's Story

"I was trying to make partner at my firm. I also was in my third trimester of pregnancy with a baby girl. Her name was to be Emma. At 38 years old, I was truly successful, happily married, and the mother of a terrific child, Elisabeth, a teen. My heart was in the right place, but my head was not.

"On a brisk fall morning I left the house for a meeting that was two hours away. I was running late. As I got into the car, my back ached and I was not feeling well. I pushed on. I reached the meeting on time, but all the way to the client site I was doing the negative internal speak we all do when we're not being kind to ourselves as women or as human beings.

"By late morning, I felt worse. As I stood in front of an all-male audience, facilitating an important planning and strategy session at the client's, I knew. I knew my darkest fear had come true. At the lunch break, I called my ob-gyn to get results of a test I had taken, which confirmed it. The fetus was dead; I had toxic shock syndrome, and I needed to go to the hospital. I didn't—for fear of losing my job, for fear of losing my client, my credibility, and my career. I chose my career over my own health. I worked on through the end of the day. I didn't get to the hospital until 8 that night!

"I'm sharing this tale in hopes of helping other women—other mothers who are dedicated, smart, and loving women—to stop treating themselves so harshly—the self-judgment, guilt, shame, blame, and other negative thinking about the impact their actions have on their careers and their overall success as working mothers."

—Cathy Greenberg

Setting Your Pace

It's easy to get swept up in the career-track mentality. Whether you're in a blue-collar or a white-collar job, you're surrounded by people who want to make manager or partner or whatever the next rung on the ladder is. At most companies, success is defined as rising through the ranks at a particular pace, earning raises and other plums, managing ever more people. Of course, the higher you go in any organization, the more demanding—and, likely, time-consuming—the work will be.

As a working mother, give yourself permission to choose the track and the timing that suits you. Don't let other people or external forces define success or your pace toward it. Maybe you want to take the slower "mommy track" for a few years while the kids are young. That doesn't mean you can never rise in the organization. It only means you will take longer to reach your goal. But you must decide for yourself if you are comfortable with that trade-off. That's the choice Fox Cable's Sherry Brennan made; Sharon Allen made the choice, too. Maybe, when you're ready to kick your career up a notch, you will choose a different employer or even strike off on your own. Even if you choose to stay home with the kids, you don't need to place limits on yourself.

On the other hand, if you want to rocket to the top as quickly as possible, go for it. Realize, though, what that decision will mean for you and your family. Time will most likely always be in short supply. If your career requires you to travel, family time will be a truly precious commodity. But if you make that choice—rather than have it imposed on you—then you are in control of your life. If you are married or have a life partner, you will need that individual's support. The working moms we talked to who made it to the top of their chosen careers all spoke of the importance of having a partner who not only supported them, but was proud of their accomplishments. Choosing your own path rather than having it imposed on you makes the hard work and inconveniences easier to bear.

A Mother's Story

"I knew I wanted to be a lawyer when I was 8 years old. My DNA was very focused on being a successful lawyer, and I was a successful lawyer.

"To my surprise, by the time I was 34, I was married to a man who loved me, and we had two kids. The husband and children had never been in my plans.

"We had a wonderful nanny who took such good care of my sons that I felt superfluous. I began to feel that my purpose in life was to make the money to pay the nanny, so the boys could be happy with her because she was a better mother than I was. The frustration built until I made a radical decision. I wanted to leave Chicago and move to Tucson. Fortunately, my company agreed to let me telecommute so that I could be a full-time lawyer and a stay-at-home mom.

"My husband was supportive, and agreed to go along with my crazy plan. It was the hardest and the best decision I've ever made. My career definitely changed course, but I still love my work and the people I work with. And I got to spend precious years with my sons, doing homework, going to their sporting events, meeting their friends.

"I will never accomplish the original professional goals that I set for myself long ago, but I have new goals now. My sons' childhoods are almost over. I'm so glad I made the choice to not miss them."

—Barrett Avigdor

Self-Doubt

Working mothers regularly doubt their decisions. They question whether they are doing the right thing for their families. Would the kids be better off if I stayed at home full-time? Am I pulling my weight at work if I leave every day at 5 to pick up the kids from day care? If you are one of those self-doubters, we have one word of advice: Stop. Trust yourself and your decisions; if you make a wrong decision, you'll fix it; you always do. Self-doubt is the great eroder. It eats away self-confidence and drains valuable energy. You don't have time for self-doubt.

To find your happiness in life, trust your instincts. You were given maternal instincts for a reason, but your other instincts are equally as valid. Listen to them. Listen to your internal voices. Trust your gut feelings. We all receive information we don't even know we're processing, but it informs our brains and bodies and instincts.

If you make a mistake every now and then, so what! Give yourself permission to make mistakes. They are signals that show you're learning, growing, experimenting, and being creative. Everybody makes mistakes. Not everyone admits them, however, because of a fear of being seen as less than perfect. If you realize upfront that you're not perfect and allow yourself to make mistakes, you'll go a long way toward being happy and free. Set the same standard for yourself that you apply to your loved ones. You cut them plenty of slack. You deserve some slack, too.

Unhappiness

Remember Tal Ben-Shahar? He's the author and psychologist who teaches a happiness course at Harvard mentioned in Chapter 1. Ben-Shahar divides unhappy people into three categories:

1. **Achievers** are the people who defer their happiness. They work very hard today, often to the point of misery, on the assumption they will be happy when . . . they get promoted, or make a million dollars, or retire. Western culture reinforces this approach because it rewards results, not processes. From the time we are children, we are taught to defer our pleasure because when we win the game, get the A, or attain whatever goal we set for ourselves, we will have earned our happiness. Then we can be happy. Too often, however, attaining the goal provides only relief, not happiness, and the need to set another goal.

2. **Pleasure seekers** look for pleasure in the moment with little thought to the future. Their lives focus on the pursuit of pleasure and the avoidance of pain. Over time, however, the lack of meaning or purpose to her pursuits makes the hedonist restless and unhappy.

3. **Those who have given up** on happiness. They are resigned to the belief that life has no meaning, and they go through life on autopilot, feeling few highs or lows, neither passion nor

despair. They suffer from the false belief that happiness is simply unattainable.

In all of our research and among our personal acquaintances, we have yet to meet a mother who is a pleasure seeker. Most pleasure seekers know that raising children is hard work, so they tend not to have any. Or when they do have children, they stop being pleasure seekers.

Many women fit the achiever model. They think they'll be happy when they reach a certain career milestone or when the children outgrow their demanding stage. What they may not appreciate is that new milestones to achieve will always be there. When the children outgrow their demanding stage, they will be heading off to college. By living too much for the future, these women lose sight of the beauty of the present.

The unhappiest working mothers are those who have given up on happiness, moving through life like robots, accomplishing a stunning array of tasks at work and at home but taking little joy in any of it. These women are too exhausted—emotionally and spiritually as well as physically—to feel joy, or much of anything else. For them, life is drudgery, something to be gotten through. They rarely experience the highs or the lows as they trudge on. They love their children and make sure they're safe, healthy, and have their homework done, but they take little joy in the time they spend with their kids. These women are caught in a never-ending list of tasks and their only focus is to cross one more chore off the list.

We hope that, after reading this book, you will cease to be any one of these archetypes. It is our hope that you will find happiness by aligning your time to your values, surrounding yourself with people who give you positive energy, and finding joy in the small moments that happen every day.

Family-Unfriendly Workplaces

If you are a working mom in the United States, you've probably felt, at least from time to time, that the rules at work are just not family friendly. You're right. The United States lags "dramatically behind all

high-income countries and many middle- and low-income countries"
when it comes to good working conditions for families, according to a
study by McGill University's Institute for Health and Social Policy.

> *I think in the United States we should do a better job of*
> *respecting holidays and vacations. It's more cultural than*
> *anything. I'd like to see a culture that respects time away*
> *from work as truly away from work, although some of*
> *that [attitude] is self-imposed.*
>
> —Jill Smart, working mother
> and chief human resources officer at Accenture

"More countries are providing the workplace protections that
millions of Americans can only dream of," said Dr. Jody Heymann,
the study's lead author, founder of the Harvard-based Project on
Global Working Families and director of the McGill Institute for Health
and Social Policy. "The U.S. has been a proud leader in adopting laws
that provide for equal opportunity in the workplace, but our work/
family protections are among the worst."

Consider a few findings from Heymann's "The 2007 Work, Family,
and Equity Index: How Does the U.S. Measure Up?"[1]

- ◆ Out of 173 countries studied, 168 guarantee paid maternity
  leave, with 98 of these countries offering 14 or more weeks of
  paid leave. The United States provides no paid leave for
  mothers. Lesotho, Liberia, Swaziland, and Papua New Guinea
  are the only other countries studied that do not guarantee leave
  with income to mothers.
- ◆ At least 107 countries protect working women's right to breastfeed, and the breaks are paid in at least 73 of those countries.
  The United States does not guarantee the right to breastfeed,
  even though breastfeeding is demonstrated to reduce infant
  mortality one-and-a-half- to five-fold.
- ◆ At least 145 countries provide paid sick days for short- or long-
  term illnesses, with 127 providing a week or more annually.
  The United States provides unpaid leave only for serious
  illnesses through the Family & Medical Leave Act, which

does not cover all workers, and has no federal law providing for paid sick days.

◆ One hundred and thirty-seven countries require employers to provide paid annual leave. The United States does not.

◆ At least 134 countries have laws that fix the maximum length of the workweek. The United States does not have a maximum workweek length or a limit on mandatory overtime per week.

These findings don't mean, however, that family-friendly companies don't exist. They do, and they thrive because such companies understand that happy employees make better employees, and that translates to the bottom line. To read about the top family-friendly companies, and what makes them that way, see *Working Mother* magazine or visit its web site.[2]

Bottom Lines: Exercises to Try

CONNECTING TO YOURSELF AND OTHERS

Ask yourself the following questions:

◆ Do I take the time I need to allow for connecting to myself, my partner, or loved ones?

◆ Do I take the time I need to allow for meaningful connections to others?

◆ How do I know when I should be focused on making connections for my well-being?

◆ What can I do to support my own networking abilities?

◆ Do I have access to the right people through my network and, if not, how can I get access to better connections?

◆ Who do I know who can help me?

◆ How can I take the first step to engage?

THE W.I.L.L. TO BE HAPPY

This is a tool to help provide insight, offer ways out of the happiness traps, and help you understand how to create your own happily ever after. Remember, the happiness traps we talked about in this chapter include:

- ◆ Supermom
- ◆ Money matters
- ◆ Whose needs
- ◆ Resentment
- ◆ I am what I do
- ◆ Self-doubt
- ◆ Setting your pace

Directions:

a. Pick the top three traps you fall into.

b. Prioritize these traps 1, 2, 3.

c. Answer the following questions:

What might trigger falling into the trap of . . . .? Complete the statement, "I know when I am in this trap when . . . (fill in the blank with an example of your behavior associated with the trap).

If you were watching yourself in the trap, what would you recommend to avoid the trap?

Let's provide some suggestions for solutions.

Link possible solutions to actions that you can take to avoid the trap.

d. What have you learned about yourself from this exercise? How can you implement it and what support will you need to do so?

e. Take action.

DAILY JOURNAL NOTES

Keeping a daily journal can help you get a grip on your happiness. You can use the following template as a starting point. If you prefer to follow your own format, think about asking yourself these questions, too.

Name: _____

Date: _____

Time: _____

◆ Relationships:
What, if any interactions, thoughts, or memories you've had today have given you energy and which have left you feeling less energized?

Energy:

How would you describe your energy today—morning, afternoon, evening?

When did it shift, and what may have affected this change?

◆ Values:
What values played a key role in your day?

Have you been faithful to your values today?

Do you feel differently when you don't keep your commitments according to your values?

◆ Happiness Traps:
What trap(s) were you able to avoid today as a result of your positive outlook and focused energy?

Chapter 6

What about the Kids?

My mom is my hero.
—Rocco "Little Rock" Fiorentino, 12, son of working mother
Tina Fiorentino, co-founder and executive director of The Little
Rock Foundation

When you're at peace and happy with your choices as a mom—
whether you go to work or stay at home—you and your children
thrive. There is not a right or a wrong choice. If you are happy to stay
home with your kids, they will thrive. If you enjoy work and the
money you earn helps create financial stability for the family that also
helps your children thrive. It's that simple. Yet the myth persists that
working mothers deprive their children of the maternal love and
attention that children need to thrive. It's simply not true.

Amy, a working mother of two, says it best, "Your happiness
shapes your kids."

Children Thrive in Happy Families

How you approach mothering is your choice. If staying at home with
your children full-time or even part-time for a few years after they're
born is what satisfies your needs and values and brings you true
happiness, that's wonderful and good. But, for millions of women,
staying home is not a viable option—either for financial reasons,
emotional reasons, or both.

Your Kids Need You to be Happy

Don't be afraid or worry that your choice to work hurts your children. It doesn't, reports the American Academy of Pediatrics. There's no scientific evidence to show that children are harmed when their mothers work, the prestigious organization said in a 2004 report. "A child's development is more influenced by the amount of stress in the family, how the family feels about the mother's working, and the quality of child care. A child who is emotionally well-adjusted, well-loved, and well-cared-for will thrive regardless of whether the mother works outside the home," according to *Caring for Your Baby and Young Child— Birth to Age 5*, a book by the American Academy of Pediatrics, edited by Steven Shelov, M.D.

About Quality

We all want our children to be emotionally well-adjusted, well-loved, and well-cared-for. Making sure we do that doesn't take a complex formula. But it does mean that when we do spend time with our children, we are mindful and conscious of the messages we convey to them directly and indirectly.

The Myth Debunked

Our biggest source of guilt as working mothers comes from this fear that we're somehow hurting our kids and they suffer because we're not with them all the time. "Guilt is the *mother card.* As a mother you always feel guilty, no matter what," says Myf, a happy working mother of three now-grown and successful children in Denver, Colorado. "But I've always had to work and I enjoy it. I'm better for it and so are my children."

As a then-single mom, Myf raised her children, worked two jobs, and earned a bachelor's degree at a local college at the same time. "My kids always saw me with my head in a textbook, and I was a great role model. We're all voracious readers now," Myf says.

Children of Working Moms Thrive

Success stories abound of children of working moms who grow up, feel loved and secure, and go on to live happy, productive lives. The popular press, however, seems to highlight negative stories about working mothers. Books and articles delve into the troubles of latchkey kids, and talk shows regularly take working mothers to task by claiming their children are harmed because their mothers leave them each day to go to work. Working mothers take the blame for everything from childhood obesity to increases in attention deficit hyperactivity disorder in kids. No wonder we feel guilty. But it's time for a reality check.

Happiness Tip: When you realize that you're not perfect and allow yourself a few mistakes, you'll go a long way toward being happy.

Authentically Happy: A Daughter's Story

Makenzie Rath is the daughter of working mother Kimberly Rath, president and co-founder of Talent Plus (www.talentplus.com), a Lincoln, Nebraska-based global human resources consulting firm. Makenzie shares her thoughts on growing up with a hard-working mother:

"A huge advantage of growing up with a working mother is that we were all extremely self-directed. My brothers and I learned how to make our own decisions very early on. For example, if I decided I wanted to get my hair cut, I would check my schedule and call to set up an appointment. In addition, we learned how to manage our time and money really well. Our mom gave us the tools to be successful, and we were expected to take those tools, put them into action, and get things done. Another big advantage was all of the travel we were able to do. We met significant businesspeople around the world and had

(continued)

many new experiences with other cultures. Within our travels, we began to see how big the world really is and how many possibilities were out there awaiting us. . . . At the end of the day it was a team effort by everyone in our family to make everything work."

As mothers, we set the tone for our families. Our happiness helps us raise happy, healthy, well-adjusted, and successful kids. Even if you are comfortable and confident in your decision to work, tough moments are inevitable. Most of us have gone through the agony—and the guilt—of trying to find day care for our children or have had to face a tearful morning good-bye. We understand the tremendous sacrifices that we as working mothers must make in sharing the care of our children with others. But if work is an important element of our happiness, then the positives for us and our children far outweigh the negatives. On the other hand, if our happiness comes from staying at home full time and if family finances allow for it, then that's the best thing we can do for ourselves and our families.

Research Discounts Claims of Damage Done to Kids by Mom Working

Children of working mothers do not develop differently from those whose mothers stay at home full time. Research discounts claims that working mothers harm their children by working.

Authentically Happy: A Son's Story

Rocco "Little Rock" Fiorentino, 12, talks about his happy working mother, Tina, co-founder, with her husband, and executive director of The Little Rock Foundation (http://tlrf.org), a nonprofit volunteer organization dedicated to improving the lives of blind and visually impaired children.

My mom doesn't have a paying job where she collects a paycheck every week, but she is paid with something much more valuable. She volunteers her time for the Little Rock Foundation, to help blind and visually impaired children like me. I have been blind since birth *[Rocco was born prematurely and given a 5 percent chance of survival!]*.

My mom is everything to me. She is a caring person and her enthusiastic nature makes her a one-of-a-kind person to me. She spends every day talking to other moms who have blind and visually impaired children, helping them to know there is hope for their child. She works hard to create new programs for blind or visually impaired kids to participate in, and I love working with her and sharing my ideas.

She always listens to what I have to say. She always has my best interests at heart. She has taught me to believe in my dreams and never give up on what is important to me. She says, "When you volunteer your time for someone in need, you are rewarded in your heart by 10 times the effort."

My mom means the world to me. My mom is my hero!

(The Philadelphia-based nonprofit Little Rock Foundation provides college scholarships and operates a camp for blind and visually impaired kids, as well as provides resource centers to help parents help their special children thrive. See and hear how music prodigy—singer, composer, and pianist—Little Rock thrives at www.musicbyrocco.com.)

The amount of time a mother spends with her child isn't as important as what she brings to the relationship, says Aletha Huston, Ph.D., the Priscilla Pond Flawn Regents Professor in Child Development at the University of Texas/Austin, and director of a 2005 study that looked at the effects of maternal employment on the development of children ages 6 months to 36 months. The study covered 1,053 mothers living in 10 locations in the United States.

"The study is one of the few to consider maternal time use during early infancy when crucial attachments to caregivers are developing," says Huston. "Infants also are thought to learn what to expect of the world from caregivers during this time, such as how much they can depend on others. The mother is an important source of care then, but she doesn't have to be there 24 hours a day to build a strong relationship with her child," she adds.[1]

Huston's findings show that employed and student mothers actually compensate for their time away from home. On average, these moms worked and/or went to school 33 hours a week, but spent more time with their children on days off, and less time on household chores, leisure, and other activities. Infants bonded equally well whether mom stayed home or worked. Neither were there differences with regard to the language development, cognitive ability, or social development of infants whose mothers worked versus those who stayed home full time.

Huston's study confirmed the results of a 1999 study by Elizabeth Harvey, Ph.D, then at the Department of Psychology, University of Connecticut, and now at the University of Massachusetts at Amherst, the findings of which appeared in the American Psychological Association's journal *Developmental Psychology.*[2] That survey involved 12,000 women and their children and followed them over two decades. Harvey also found that children whose mothers worked during the first three years of their lives were not significantly different from those whose mothers did not work. Children whose mothers worked long hours did have slightly lower scores on tests that measure vocabulary and individual student achievement. But those differences were small and faded over time. In fact, the study reports, "There was some support for the hypothesis that parental employment positively affects children's development by increasing family income."

Working Guilt

Estelle, a 40-something mother of an 11-year-old, still vividly remembers a morning when her daughter, who never cried, was still a toddler. "I had just dropped her off at day care and closed the door, when she literally threw herself at the closed door. I could hear her wailing and pounding on that door. I felt like my heart was ripped out of my chest. I knew Anna was upset because she hadn't slept much the night before and wasn't feeling well, but it still tore at my heart."

Most of us probably have faced a traumatic good-bye—and the guilt that comes with it—like Estelle did. But for every one of those tearful moments, we also likely can remember a happy moment, too. Every day when Tara drops Sam at day care, the little girl is so excited. "She's out the door with a wave and a cheerful, 'Bye Mommy,' before I can close the car door," says Tara. "She loves to see me in the afternoon, too, and comes running, throws her arms around me, and always tells me she missed me."

Claudia recalls how enriching preschool was for her son. "When Max was in preschool, I felt guilty until the first parent/teacher night. My 4-year-old son took me by the hand and proudly showed me how he had mastered every puzzle and math game in the room. Then he introduced me to his teachers and every child in the room. They called him 'The Mayor of Montessori.' I knew he never would have learned that much staying home with me."

Liz, a working mother of four in Delaware, offers her own sage advice to avoid the traumatic good-bye and any pangs of guilt associated with it: "Never drop off, always pick up." Liz's husband is the designated parent to drop off the kids in the morning. Fathers and their children don't generally feel the same intensity of emotion when they say good-bye as children and mothers feel, says Liz, so why not take advantage of that?

Stay-at-Home Guilt

We seldom hear about it, but stay-at-home moms feel guilty, too. It's simply a part of being a mother, and studies prove it. Ninety-five percent of women say they experience feelings of guilt as mothers, according to *Mommy Guilt: Learn to Worry Less, Focus on What Matters Most, and Raise Happier Kids*, by J. Bort, A. Pflock, and D. Renner

(New York: AMACOM, 2005). The authors talked with hundreds of mothers then analyzed their responses for the book.

As moms, our kids love us and miss us when we are not with them, and we love and miss them too. That's why a working mother—or any mother—feels sad when she misses a school function or an after-school event. But the guilt comes from somewhere else.

Lori, mother of three—ages 2, 4, and 8—is a 30-something stay-at-home mom. "I go to the gym and work out every day. The kids go to day care. I have a great lady I take them to. I feel bad, but it's my sanity, if you know what I mean."

Unrealistic Expectations

Many of us grew up in the United States with the stay-at-home mom as the perfect American ideal. TV gave us cultural icons of stay-at-home moms like June Cleaver (*Leave It to Beaver*) and Jane Jetson (*The Jetsons*). These were moms on a pedestal, glorified and idolized for their perfection, and we believed we were supposed to be like them. If your mother worked, you may have resented it and thought it would have been better for her to stay at home like everyone else's mom. That's the conditioning of American society. Other cultures give fathers and the extended family a much bigger role in child-rearing. In those cultures, working mothers feel less guilt because the expectations of them are more realistic.

Sofia, 33, is a working mother in Buenos Aires and shares the responsibility of child care 50/50 with her husband. She also has a nanny, and her mother and mother-in-law pitch in, too. Maria, 42, also from Buenos Aires, doesn't have a nanny, but she also splits child-raising responsibilities "50-50 or 60-40" with her husband (he picks up the biggest share). On the other side of the world in Shanghai, Kathy, 40, is a working mother of two whose husband travels. For child care she has a nanny and "sometimes relatives come and stay for months to help."

We're emphasizing the importance of spending quality time with your kids. Some people tend to distort that idea and suggest it means spending every minute with your children playing educational games

Authentically Happy

Heather was a stay-at-home mom with her three children for 10 years. Although Heather's mom had been a stay-at-home mom, Heather and her two sisters always felt that they were expected to achieve and to give back to the community in a meaningful way.

"I thought I had to be my father and my mother," Heather says. Heather loved being the primary caregiver for her children, but a big part of her felt unfulfilled staying at home. With a law degree from Harvard and a highly successful and philanthropic family, Heather believed that her purpose in life was something different from solely raising her children. Her frustration built over the years and spilled over into her marriage. "I tried not to let the kids feel my frustration but I know it made me irritable with them sometimes," she says.

When her youngest started preschool, Heather began to volunteer at the office of her state senator. Before she knew it, she was asked to run for a state senate seat. The campaign was a big family project—the kids loved campaigning for their mom—but Heather felt guilty that it took her away from home so many evenings.

Now, as a state senator, Heather loves her work. She feels she is doing what she was meant to do and her family is proud of her accomplishments. Heather spends one-third of her time in the state capitol, away from home. The rest of the time, she is able to send the kids off to school in the morning and can usually be home when they get home from school. She is sad when she has to miss school or athletic events, but says, "I'm so much happier now that I feel I'm a better mom than I was when I was home full time and frustrated. I admire mothers who can stay home full time and find their fulfillment in that. It just wasn't me."

and using flash cards. Conversely, others distort the idea to mean that a half-hour of high-quality time with a child is just as good as spending the whole day. As with so much related to raising children, the answer is individual and comes down to balance and common sense.

Without a doubt, young children would love to have their mothers with them 24 hours a day 7 days a week. Being constantly present and available to your children, however, is draining on any woman, and isn't always the best thing for the child, either. Mothers, whether they work or not, need time for themselves to reenergize so they can be the best they can for their children. It's tough to be a role model for happiness if you're too exhausted to be happy yourself.

A "Good Mother"—Defined

What is a "good" mother? We asked hundreds of working women that question. Here are a few of their answers:

- ◆ A good mother is someone who prepares her kids to do better than she did in the world—better in terms of achievement and in doing good. Showing them how to be self-sufficient, kind, being the best person they can be, and learning how to be happy. A good mother knows she is not responsible for her children's happiness.—Nancy, mother of two, Chicago, Illinois
- ◆ A good mother is someone who achieves what she would like to achieve. She is nurturing, present, willing to make compromises, loving. It doesn't take a lot of money to be a good mother. It takes love and consistency, emotional connection, nurturing. A good mother gives her children support and love.—Debra, mother of two, Tucson, Arizona
- ◆ A good mother is present, nurturing, supportive, in control, and reliable (she will be there when needed, no matter what). She teaches her children to be thoughtful and good people. She gives love freely, saying "I love you" a lot, no matter what. She holds her children accountable for their actions. She teaches them hard life lessons. She is always honest.—Julie, mother of two, Tucson, Arizona
- ◆ A good mom is someone who knows how to and does help her kids become the best version of them. Teaching them values— shaping them, giving them values—making them good human

beings. You don't have to be a stay-at-home or working mom to do that.—Robin, mother of three, Chicago, Illinois

◆ A good mother protects but doesn't overprotect her children. She is affectionate. She accompanies her child in his development. She allows her child to grow. She teaches by example. Gives love, security, and tranquility.—Sofia, mother of two, Buenos Aires, Argentina

◆ A good mother is a person who understands the needs of her particular child. She is a safe haven but not so overly protective that she gets in the way of her children experiencing life. She makes her children feel loved and protected. She acts as a role model for her children, showing them that life is full of possibilities.—Yaarit, mother of two, Atlanta, Georgia

"Real" mothers are those who are true to their own values and who do the powerful and simple things to raise children who are confident, self-sufficient, and joyful, says Michele Borba, Ed.D., in her book *12 Simple Secrets Real Moms Know: Getting Back to Basics and Raising Happy Kids* (Jossey-Bass, 2006). Borba also describes good moms as those who know how to give and receive unconditional love. They are the moms who find their own happiness so they can bring joy into their homes.

In her book, Borba offers more observations of what it means to be a "real" mother:

◆ "Real mothers are happier and have more joy in their families because there is so much less pretense and putting on to keep up."

◆ "Real moms are less guilty and anxious because they're not trying to be perfect by other people's standards."

◆ "Real moms are more appreciated because their kids have had a chance to know their interests and passions."

Working is an essential part of finding happiness for many women. For some of us, the intellectual stimulation of work helps us feel alive and fulfilled; for others, it's the feeling of being useful, of contributing to someone or something beyond our families. Even if a mother doesn't need to work for financial reasons, many do so because they like the financial independence that work affords them, and that independence becomes an essential element in their happiness. For the very lucky few women who have found their life's purpose and who feel that their work is helping them to fulfill that purpose, their happiness is completely entwined with their work.

Because we as mothers are the center of the family unit and our mood sets the tone for our children and significant others, we owe it to ourselves and our families to find our happiness.

Is Less More?

Have you ever thought about how you would like your children to remember you when they're grown? Will it be as a comfortable parent who always listened and offered guidance when asked or as a frantic mother who shuttled the kids from practice to lessons to competition?

A Mother's Story: Home Cooking

A senior HR executive at a leading health-care company shared a story about how she wanted her children to remember her when she took a break from work during her kids' formative years.

With the luxury of a brief downtime between jobs, Kathy looked forward to making a meal from scratch daily for her husband and two children in the hopes they would have happy memories of their stay-at-home mom.

One day Kathy was running a little late coming home from an appointment and thought about how she could keep up her mommy points with the family and provide that homemade experience despite being short on time. She saw a Boston Market restaurant, and pulled in to pick up dinner for the family.

Safely at home before the children, Kathy carefully emptied each container of mashed potatoes, gravy, vegetables, biscuits, and the rotisserie chicken into her own cookware. When the table was finally ready, it looked as if she had slaved all day in the kitchen, cooking with love. Kathy was happy to serve the take-out dinner without making it obvious that it wasn't homemade.

As her son and daughter dug into the mashed potatoes and gravy, they smiled and said, "Mom this is so good, you should make this all the time." Kathy was overjoyed that the kids had no idea that she actually had stopped and picked up the meal with just as much love as she had served it. What she could not do was give away her secret and disappoint the children. For years, she never let them know that they had eaten Boston Market takeout that night or any subsequent night because Kathy said it never really mattered. What mattered was that the family enjoyed an evening meal together, not who actually made the food.

Kathy eventually went back to work and always remembered that her children enjoyed the idea of eating meals at home together more than the fact that the meals were homemade.

Kathy's kids are college-age today, but she still laughs at the pressure she put on herself to be the perfect stay-at-home mom. Now the kids show up on weekends and holidays with pillow-cases full of laundry and the hope of a home-cooked meal with Mom and Dad. Now that they are on their way to being successful adults they truly appreciate the extra bit of time they have with Mom and Dad. They especially enjoy that home-cooked meal, which, Kathy admits, is often a combination of home preparation and takeout. The happiness comes from a family meal together, not who cooks it!

Statistics show that the American lifestyle of cramming our children's schedules full of activities and classes isn't making them happy and appreciative but stressed and sad, instead. The communications gap is widening, too. Let's look at a few statistics compiled from government and private organizations:

◆ Teen suicide rates climbed 39 percent between 1970 and 2004, according to Child Trends, a nonprofit, nonpartisan research center that studies children at all states of development.[3]

- In 2003, 29 percent of all students in grades 9 to 12 reported feeling sad or hopeless almost every day for an extended period—two or more weeks in a row.[4]
- Eighty-two percent of 12- to 15-year-olds, and 67 percent of 8- to 11-year-olds say at least some of the time they keep things from their parents because they think they just "won't understand," according to "The Nickelodeon/Talking with Kids National Survey of Parents and Kids."[5]
- Based on our focus groups, an overwhelming number of parents would like to spend more time with their kids, and kids want more time with their parents.

We do all those things out of love for our children and our desire to help them succeed. What our kids and these statistics are telling us is that the best thing we can do for them is to find our own happiness and peace and to share that sense of calm and joy with them.

Helping Your Kids Flourish

Parenting is a lot like managing people at work. Good parenting and good management go hand-in-hand. We're not suggesting that raising a family is a business, but it is important to set high goals for your family—your team—to be supportive of them, and to allow your children to grow, develop, and learn to become independent human beings.

Mothers, as we mentioned, are the CEOs of the family and set the emotional tone for their households. We also know, from the work of Barbara L. Fredrickson, Ph.D. (Kenan Distinguished Professor of Psychology and principal investigator of the Positive Emotions and Psychophysiology Lab at the University of North Carolina), that human beings flourish when they are surrounded by "positivity." Flourishing describes the state in which people do their best work, when they are most creative and productive. As leaders at work, we seek to help our teams flourish. According to Fredrickson's research, when we experience three positive emotions for every one negative emotion, we become more creative and a better version of ourselves. Anything less than the 3:1 ratio doesn't work.

This is the recipe for human flourishing and it works for anyone at any age. (That's why smart employers create very positive and supportive work environments in order to stimulate the creativity of their people.) Parents will want to do the same for their children, and create an environment at home where their children can flourish. That means commenting on all the things they do right as well as noting the things you'd like them to do differently. And, of course, telling them you love them often and without any particular reason.

Parents are role models for the kind of people they would like their children to be. If you want your children to be happy adults, it's important to show them how a happy adult lives. Just as the CEO needs to demonstrate the core values of his company, you need to do the same if you want your children to live in accordance with your values. If you want your children to find joy in the simple things of life, you need to find it yourself, and share that joy with them every day. The choices you make every day between joy and guilt, between calm and frenzy, between self-love and self-criticism, are choices you also are making for your children. Rather than saying to your daughter, "Don't make the same mistakes I did," show her how you are able to bounce back from those mistakes and get your life on a track that brings you happiness.

> *Your kids watch what you do. If your work makes you feel*
> *happy and fulfilled, your kids will see and understand that.*
> —Barrett Avigdor

Role Models

If you want to teach your children how to take care of themselves, be independent, and follow their passion, then you should do the same. If that means you work outside the home to fulfill an important part of your own life, then working is part of your mothering. It doesn't detract from it; it adds to it.

Genevieve Bos, co-founder of PINK and a "virtual" mom for the many women she helps in business and in life, recalls a story about the female president of Iceland and the importance of how we see ourselves as women.

A long line of boys would accumulate outside her meetings for the purpose of asking her one question. Could a boy be president? It never dawned on her that the power of the mirror held up to these young boys could have caused such a dilemma. Boys under the age of 18 had known only a woman as president of their country.

If you stay home full time to take care of your kids and feel like a martyr because you're doing so, you teach your children that your needs and desires are less important than theirs, and that's the role you model for their future. It also is likely to make them feel guilty if they cannot live up to your expectations. After all, if you sacrificed your happiness for them, they may feel they owe you an enormous debt they need to repay rather than pursue what makes them happy.

On the other hand, if you do what you truly desire—whether that means staying at home or going to work—you teach your children to follow their passion and to make their contribution in the way they feel is most important. That frees them to do the same. And it is by following their passion that they're most likely to find their own happiness.

Authentically Happy

Kim Martin, mother of two daughters, loves her work and thrives on its intellectual and social stimulation. She can't ever imagine retiring, says the president and general manager of WE tv. Her daughters, born while Kim worked for The Discovery Channel, don't want her to retire, either. In fact, her youngest wants her current job when she grows up and keeps telling her mom to hold it open for her!

The girls can't wait to go to college and then into business, too.

Happiness Compass

We teach our children values and how to act on those values by living our lives consistently with our own values. If we stand for something, we give our children moral compasses to guide them on their own life journeys and shape them into the kind of adults we want them to be.

We also should teach our children how to maintain their own level of happiness. Being aware that they are responsible for their own happiness is a key to their success as well-rounded adults. By helping our children understand that happiness is a choice they can make every day, we support their own awareness about happiness and possibly even help them achieve more control over their long-term outlook on happiness. Teaching our children about a happiness compass, including what happiness is, what it means for them, and how they can contribute to their happiness as adults, could go a long way toward shaping our children's lives for success.

Self-Coaching Break: Real Family Values

Michele Borba, Ed.D., in her book *12 Simple Secrets Real Moms Know: Getting Back to Basics and Raising Happy Kids* (Jossey-Bass, 2006) suggests sitting down with your family to discuss what the family wants to stand for—the values that are important to the family.

She then suggests you agree as a family to a project or set of actions that support those values. For example, if helping those less fortunate is a value, choose a charity that the family can get involved in and decide how you will participate in that charity—perhaps by raising money or volunteering your time.

Statistics suggest that too many parents talk the talk but may not live in accordance with their values. In a 2004 survey of more than 24,700 high school students, 66 percent said they cheat on exams, and 93 percent said it is important to be a person with good character.[6] Somehow, the point was lost on those kids that people with good character should not cheat on exams.

At work and at home, teaching values also means it's important to set rules that are clear, fair, and consistently enforced. We live in a society in which instant gratification is the rule, not the exception. It sometimes feels as if no one else in the neighborhood has rules, and who wants to be accused of being the meanest parent in the world or told they are totally out of touch? Yet, in your heart—and likely in your child's heart, too—you know right from wrong and you should set rules for your children that are consistent with your own moral compass. You're not hurting your child; you're helping nurture a moral framework for their lives. That moral framework is a happiness compass that is an important component for a future life of happiness.

Teach Your Child to Love Him/Herself

Learning to love and accept ourselves for who we are is part of embracing our own happiness. Understanding who your child is and helping him to build on his strengths will help him to love and accept himself, too. There's such terrific pressure on kids to be perfect. As we encourage our children to push themselves to be their best, we must always remind them that we love them for who they are—not what they've accomplished. It's much easier to do that for your children if you also do it for yourself. You are far more than the sum of your accomplishments or the size of your paycheck. As you learn to love yourself for who you are, with your imperfections and limitations, you teach your children to do the same.

In the process of helping them love who they are by pointing out their strengths and talents in the face of imperfection, you build on their capacity to flourish. The result is a more highly developed sense of life satisfaction, which ultimately contributes to increased happiness.

In her book *Your Child's Strengths* (Viking Penguin, 2008), Jenifer Fox, an educator and head of a school in New Jersey, makes a compelling argument that standardization in schools and our emphasis on test scores is getting in the way of our children truly learning and finding what they are passionate about. As parents, our contribution to our children's education can be to help them find what they love to do.

Mothers—whether they work or not—who truly see their children for who they are and instill in them a love of learning and nurture them to be their own unique persons, are the mothers who help their children feel comfortable and confident with themselves.

> *I'm really good at the things that are important to me, like sports and school. I'm not that good at other things, like music. That's okay because no one is good at everything.*
> —Harrison, age 13

Encourage Independence and Self-Reliance

We all want our kids to grow up as independent and self-reliant adults. Yet, the number of 26-year-olds living at home has doubled since 1970. It may be that we, as mothers, do too much for our kids. With the best intentions, we are so focused on the outcome rather than the process that we are teaching our kids to rely on us and not on themselves. When we do their homework or prepare them for a test, and we sometimes foster an unhealthy dependence that makes them feel as if they can't succeed without our help.

Children of working moms can often be more self-sufficient. Just ask them: "If your mom is working and you're at home, you have to do your homework on your own. It teaches you to be more motivated and independent," says Daniel, 13, whose mother works part time. Matt, also 13, whose mother has her own CPA firm, agrees. "Having a working mom helps at school because some kids with stay-at-home moms get tutors or their moms help them with homework. Because my mom works, I have to do my own homework so I learn more."

Acceptance

As mothers we love our children for who they are, not who we think they should be. That's not just a mantra for working moms; that's a mantra for all moms and dads. We need that mantra because we live in a competitive world in which many adults, perhaps unhappy or a little disappointed in their own lives, tend to compete through their children. They live vicariously through their kids. It's everywhere and anyone who has ever attended one of their kid's sporting events has seen it.

Even if your child is not the most gifted or the most beautiful, you share something unique with your child that you have with no one else anywhere on the planet. As a mother, the bond you have with each of your children is an opportunity and an invitation to give and to receive unconditional love. To love someone simply for who she is, for the fact of her existence, to love her with all her quirks and flaws is an extraordinary gift for both the giver and the receiver. It's pure and simple joy.

Unconditional Love

Parenting is a lot like managing people at work, with one big difference—unconditional love.

Mothers of young babies soon realize that their baby knows them by their scent, the sound of their voice, and the feel of their arms. Knowing that you can soothe your baby better than anyone simply because you are you is an astonishing revelation. As imperfect as we may feel as mothers, that bond is always there.

By showing our children unconditional love, we teach them to love themselves, a skill they need to live their own happy lives. We also allow them to love us unconditionally. Unconditional love is a very rare commodity. We get it from our parents and from our children.

Modeling Joy

We teach our children to be joyful by being joyful ourselves. As mothers, we know we are role models for our children; we know they are watching us all the time. We want them to be happy, so why would we not appreciate the importance of finding joy ourselves and sharing it with them?

Authentically Happy: Two Daughters' Stories

Kelsie, 15, and Jaylyn, 11, describe what they love about their mom, Tammie, and her work as a dialysis technician:

◆ "My mom smiles a lot and she makes people laugh."—Kelsie

◆ "My mom helps people by making sure they do not pass away. She also helps their families understand how to help as well. My mom loves her job."—Jaylyn

Joy doesn't require a long vacation or an expensive resort. You can find joy with your children in the smallest things—stopping for a special treat on the way home from school or playing board games together on a Saturday night. If you need some ideas for what would be fun, ask your children. *USA Today* polled 84,000 students in 2000, and two-thirds of them between grades 6 and 12 said they would like to spend more time with their parents. They wanted relaxed time to spend with their parents, not stress-filled discussions about grades or the logistics of soccer, then piano, then ballet classes.

Think of the time you spend with your children as if it were pearls. Each happy moment you share is a pearl that you string together in a necklace. Not every moment will be perfect. But don't be discouraged by arguments and hectic schedules—keep trying to make at least one pearl a day.

Marshall Goldsmith tried an experiment a few years ago to help him spend more time with his kids. Goldsmith is a world-renowned executive coach and best-selling author (his books include *What Got You Here Won't Get You There: How Successful People Become Even More Successful*, Hyperion). Goldsmith made sure that he and each of his kids had one-on-one time every week, and actually scheduled it into his work calendar. After three years of improving his "level of service" to his children, he checked in to see how he was doing. Both his son and daughter—now in high school—said, "You know Dad, you did a great job. We really love you, but we want to spend more time with our friends now!"

> *Because my mom works, I don't take her for granted like I would if she was home all the time. When she comes home from a business trip, I always feel really happy and I appreciate her more.*
>
> —Harrison, age 13

From the Kids' Perspective

Plenty of people talk about the "harm" children of working mothers suffer, and how society often takes us to task for pursuing our values and dreams. So we thought we should give kids of working mothers the opportunity to talk about what they see as the positives and the negatives of having a working mom, whether they like it that mom works or not, and how they might feel different or slighted compared with their friends whose moms stay at home.

Most kids talked about the good things and the happiness in their lives and with their families because their moms work. They like the fact that working makes their moms so happy and fulfilled. They also talk about the strong love and special relationship they have with their moms, and the unique ways she nurtures them.

Authentically Happy: A Son's Story

Alex, 17, has grown up with a mom who works full time. Here are his thoughts on the good and the bad of a working mom as well as why he thinks he's a better young man because his mom works.

"When I was 5, I wished my mom didn't work. I liked being with her and we always had fun together. I didn't like my teachers much then, either, so I would have rather stayed home with my mom. My mom would leave before I woke up and come home an hour before my bedtime. We had a really good nanny who would keep me distracted, but I still missed my mom.

"Now that I'm older, I have a different perspective. My mom works to make money, give the family a better life, and keep her in tune with reality. It's healthy to work. I think the disadvantages of having a stay-at-home mom outweigh the advantages. Stay-at-home moms have a hard time letting their kids grow up. Having a working mom makes you more independent. You have to learn to cope with other people because your mom is not always around. The worst thing about having a mom who works is not being able to see her all the time. She's not there to talk to all the time. Sometimes, if she comes home stressed-out about work, we don't have that much fun together.

"If my mom hadn't worked, I'd probably be less independent and wouldn't be able to cope with my problems as well. I'm more relaxed about going away to college because my mom travels a lot, so I'm used to being without her.

"I've visited a lot of cool places because my mom gets so many free miles when she travels for work. All that has definitely shaped who I am.

"When I get married and have kids, I'll want my wife to work. She deserves to work, and it would be good to have the extra money. My advice to a woman who is deciding whether to work or stay at home as a mom would be to work. It's good for adults to work. "

Kids, especially younger kids, love having their mom around and they miss their moms when they go to work. But the older kids we talked to realize that the benefits of having a mom who works, ranging from their mom's happiness to financial gains, and the fact they as kids they feel stronger and more independent. They know their moms love them, and they are proud their mothers have successful lives outside the home. Kids, no matter their ages, also liked the financial benefits and security that a working mom helps to provide.

In their own words:

- "It's not just about money. Because my mom works, we get to do lots of things together. The only bad thing is when I was little and couldn't reach the crackers, and my mom would be too busy to reach them for me."— Emma, 11
- "Working mothers don't *not* love their kids. Having a working mom, I feel more loved. She is working to benefit us."—Matt, 13
- "My mom can't always be there, but my dad and grandma are. And my mom's our Girl Scout leader, so it's okay."—Megan, 10
- "I didn't like having to go to boarding school during the week. But I got to do all sorts of great things like travel everywhere because my mom worked."—Lis, now 27, whose single mom worked while she was growing up
- "I wish she didn't work because we have to say bye when she goes to work. I think the hardest part of my mom's life is her job. She's afraid she might lose her job. It makes her feel sad. If she loses her job, we may not be able to go to Hawaii in the summer. I really want to go to Hawaii."—Robert, 7
- "I don't get much time with my mom, so when I spend time with her, I feel good and I feel like I give her comfort. I never wish she didn't work."—Philip, 10
- "I'm happy that she does what she likes. My mom tells me she likes her job every day."—Jonah, 14
- "The only difference [between me and kids whose moms stay at home] is that kids whose moms stay home are home more and can do more things for their kids like clean the house, cook, and drive their kids places. My mom works at home so it's just like having a stay-at-home mom.—Victoria, 10
- "I think the hardest part of mom's life is that she really likes to work and would probably work a lot more if she didn't have me and my brother to take care of."—Harrison, 13
- "The hardest part of my mom's life is not spending time with her kids. Struggling with her work and paying lots of bills is also hard."—Philip, 10

◆ "My advice to parents is to spend time with your kids and try to have certain hours with your job."—Veronica, 11

◆ "Going to before- and after-school care isn't the best. But me and my friends have lots of fun. And Dad or Mom picks me up early sometimes when they can, too. We have a blast on the weekends. We get to go everywhere and do lots of things."—Sierra, 12

◆ "I know my mom loves me because she tells me every day, she comes to my games, she asks where I'm going and who I'm with."—Alex, 17

Makenzie Rath, in her senior year at the University of Nebraska, knows that her mom, Kimberly Rath, is happy as a mother and in her career as president and co-founder of Talent Plus, a Nebraska-based global human resources consultancy.

"My mom's biggest strength would be her resourcefulness and her ability to always find a solution. She works very hard and is extremely dedicated to all that she does in life. . . . Yes, she is happy! She is happy when she is celebrating the success of others, when we [her kids] are successful, when she can see things that she has done or worked on come together," Makenzie says. "She is very good at never losing sight of the end goal, while also relishing in the journey along the way. She is happy when she can spend quality time with the people she loves and cares about, too."

Bottom Lines: Exercises to Try

DEVELOPING STRENGTHS: FROM SUCCESS TO SATISFACTION

At least twice a year, in a relaxed atmosphere, try this exchange with each of your children one at a time. Give each child a turn to respond, and always express your interest without judging their responses.

(continued)

Ask the question, "What do you love to do—at school, at home, with family, and with friends"?

See if a pattern emerges in their answers that helps direct your attention to your children's strengths. Our job as parents is to learn our children's strengths, and then help them build on those strengths for a lifetime of turning success into satisfaction by applying them.

QUALITY TIME

Try scheduling time into your weekly schedule with your children, your partner, and for yourself. Informal studies have shown that when busy moms treat their families, and themselves, with the importance they would give a client or customer, they actually are able to make time more effectively and more consistently for those they love and themselves. While this might not feel right at first, recognizing that you have taken the time to treat your family and yourself with the same respect you give strangers starts to feel right. Soon you will find a regular place in your busy agenda for those you really care about.

Try clearing the calendar on a Saturday or Sunday and agreeing that you and your kids will stay home and hang out together for the afternoon.

Look for an activity that appeals to you and your kids.

You are creating those childhood memories of you that your children will carry with them forever. As crazy as life is, you can make time for a story and a cuddle or a game of scrabble.

Chapter 7

When the Going Gets Tough, Get Support

*My girls are the first thing I think about when I wake up
and the last thing I think about when I go to sleep . . . .
Often I think how nice it would be to have a cloning
machine.*

—First Lady Michelle Obama, on the campaign trail July 28,
2008, Chicago, Illinois

As human beings we're innately resilient and programmed for survival. We may no longer be cavemen fending off wolf packs on the prowl, but we nonetheless are programmed to survive the challenges of today, whether in the workplace, at home, or beyond. For mothers, the survival instinct is especially strong, rising from the depths of our being as nurturers and protectors of our children. It's how we're wired as a mother regardless of whether we work or stay at home full time with our kids.

Happiness Has Real Results

One in five working women suffers anxiety or depression, according to a 2004 study by Leger Marketing for Wyeth Canada. Yet in that same study, three of four women indicate they believe

(continued)

---

it's possible to be completely symptom free. Of those women who achieved that remission from their depression/anxiety:

- ◆ 87 percent said they were 90 to 100 percent more productive.
- ◆ 86 percent were more motivated.
- ◆ 84 percent were more efficient in their jobs.
- ◆ 79 percent felt less overwhelmed at work.
- ◆ 75 percent improved their quality of work in general.

Source: Courtesy Canadian Mental Health Association[1]

Each of us has different values and parenting styles, but we're programmed for whatever it takes for our children to survive. That programming occasionally may get briefly overridden when, as working mothers, we allow ourselves to be overwhelmed by the stresses and draining strains of everything from kids to school to workplace, relationships, finances, struggles, and more. But, inevitably, the mother card takes control. We take on the challenges, we are fighters, and we are winners by nature. When we make the right choices, embracing our values and all the wonderful things in our lives, our kids are winners, too.

Happiness Tip: Set the same standards for yourself that you apply to your loved ones; cut yourself the same slack you give others.

A Balancing Act

The hundreds of working mothers we interviewed who, day in and day out, balance their work, children, and families despite difficult circumstances and hardships are testament to our strength and courage as women. Single moms, married moms, or moms in a relationship, many of these are working mothers whose spirits and values triumph over seemingly impossible odds. Many have had to overcome horrific sadness and trauma, yet all have learned to forgive, and to embrace happiness and joy.

Spell the word "happy," and try not to smile!
—Cathy Greenberg

The challenges we face in life bring out the best in all of us as women and as mothers, no matter the circumstances and no matter our jobs. We don't always anticipate where the journey will take us, but all of us can learn how to make the best of our difficulties.

Jessica Wright is a decorated major general in the U.S. Army National Guard—she's a recipient of the Legion of Merit. The 35-year military veteran is also a mother—her son is in college—and a wife—she's been married for 26 years. Looking at herself and her successes in life, Wright says, "I have been a mother, wife, and soldier, in that order."

Throughout her career and life, Wright has counted on mentors in the form of ex-Viet Nam veteran aviators. Her family has been there, too. During her pregnancy, she actually lived with her brother because her husband was stationed overseas. Wright also has followed the words of wisdom she learned from her mother: "People will give you a chance if you let them; what you do with that chance is up to you."

The Importance of Support

Many families have children with special needs. Mothers who have children with special challenges—physical or mental—actually spend the equivalent of one additional full day on the job of caring for that child every week—that's an additional 20 percent per day increase in workload. That doesn't mean, though, that we have to sacrifice our happiness. It's simply all the more reason to recognize that our strength lies in the wisdom recognizing the importance of a support system. You can't do it alone. Physiologically, we're programmed to turn to other women for support, too. Remember the landmark UCLA study on hormonal stress responses in women mentioned in Chapter 2? When we're stressed, our natural tendency to care for our offspring and befriend other women produces hormones that reduce our stress levels.

Self-Coaching Break: Create Your Support Network

It isn't always easy to ask others for help. To help you create your own support network, ask yourself the following questions:

- What limiting beliefs or thoughts do I need to release in order to become comfortable asking for help?
- Who in my life is good at utilizing a support system, and what do I admire about them?
- How would I feel if I were completely supported and nurtured by a robust support network? How different would my life look?

WHERE TO TURN

If you're new to a community or just need to start building a network, here are some suggestions of places to start:

- **Neighborhood community center:** It may have programs appropriate for your kids. Even if it can't help with day care, after-school activities or sports programs on the weekends can be a good way to meet other moms with kids the same age. Those moms may become part of your network.
- **College or university:** If there's a college or university in your area, try posting an opening for a babysitter or a group topic of interest for other working mothers on one of its electronic or physical bulletin boards. Both the working moms who are on the campus and students can respond.
- **After-school sports or other activities:** Make a point of chatting with other parents of kids who also are participants. If you get friendly enough, they may help you carpool to practices and games.
- **Family members:** If they don't work, they may be willing to watch your kids if they have to stay home from school when you have to work.

- ◆ **Mommy and Me or Mother's Morning Out classes:** If you have very young children, enroll your kids in such classes or events as a way to meet other moms.
- ◆ **Play dates:** Arrange play dates with children who your children like. When the mother or father drops off the kids, invite the parent in for coffee and a chat to get to know him or her a little.

A Mother's Story

Jill Smart is a success personally as a mother—she has two kids, ages 16 and 11—and professionally as chief human resources officer at Accenture. An essential part of her success is the support system she has and her willingness to ask for help.

"I have a great partner. I could not do what I do and be a good mom without my husband. It's not just because he helps me. He gives me the latitude to be the working mom I want to be. He respects the choices I've made—he doesn't make me feel guilty. He makes me better.

"I'm not afraid to ask for help—at work and at home. I know my weaknesses and that helps me be a better mom. I outsource everything I can that's not related to my kids. My nanny does not do homework with my kids or take them to the doctor or bake them a cake—that's my job. But, I haven't vacuumed in 20 years. I'm not afraid to sometimes say, 'I can't be on that call because I have to go to my child's school to work at the pizza lunch.' By telling them (fellow employees) I'm going to be with my kids, I give them permission to do the same.

"Some years ago I would have taken the call and cancelled going to school. As a senior leader in the company, I think it's my responsibility to let people know we are human and we have to make the same choices they do. I have a responsibility to make it okay for men and women to have a life. It's not just about kids—it could be running a race or taking a dog to a dog show.

"A lot of women throw in the towel without trying. They don't try to be working moms because they think they can't do it."

Special Needs Kids

Remember Danielle, the salon co-owner with three sons whose picture-perfect life came crashing down when her then-successful husband, Keith, succumbed to drug abuse? Despite seeing the destruction of the man she had loved since high school, Danielle chose to focus on the joy in life—her children, their deep love for one another, her work, her friends, and her family—rather than wallow in the tragedy. Danielle believed in the abundance in her life and happily triumphed.

But that's not the whole story. Danielle's unbridled enthusiasm for life and her ability to embrace its happiness were instrumental in steering her and her children around huge obstacles. After she locked her then-drug-addicted husband out of the house to protect the kids, Danielle was on her own for two years. She and her sons had little money but loads of love and a solid system of strength and support in Danielle's parents, mother-in-law, family, and friends. Her family and friends didn't judge her, says Danielle; they helped and advised her, were always there for her, and "kept me sane."

Because her eldest son has the neurological disorder Tourette's syndrome, he needed special care and has experienced some tough times while growing up. Although the family was struggling financially, Danielle did her best to get her son the tutors and therapists he needed. Every day after work, she spent hours with him helping him focus on his homework and teaching him to accept his disorder. Danielle's determination was unwavering, as was her support for her children, no matter the odds. They thrived. Today when kids tease him about his facial tics, he says, "Yeah, I'm ticking. That's just what I do."

"If you are not happy with yourself, you can't be happy," says Danielle. "You need to get to a point where you don't care what people think and you gain confidence."

A GREATER CALLING

Tina Fiorentino understands a mother's undaunted determination to help her offspring no matter the odds, too. She's Rocco's mom, who we mentioned in the previous chapter. Tina didn't start out as a working mother. But after Little Rock was born, her life changed;

her child's survival was at stake, and she grew to recognize that her true fulfillment was to be found beyond simply staying at home to raise her child. Tina and her husband founded the nonprofit Little Rock Foundation so that other parents of visually impaired children might never have to experience the despair and disappointment and struggles she endured simply because she wanted to raise her child, who happened to have a disability.

A Mother's Story

Tina Fiorentino was 35, and her husband, Rocco Sr., 41, when Tina delivered premature twin boys four months early. (They never tried to have more children.) One of the tiny babies died, and the other, Rocco Jr., "Little Rock," was diagnosed with retinopathy of prematurity (ROP), which can, and did in his case, cause blindness. The doctors held out little hope for Little Rock's survival.

But Tina refused to give up, and instead decided she was going to raise her child to thrive as a normal, wonderful, happy, well-adjusted human being who just happened to be blind. She stayed in the hospital for six months waiting for Little Rock to be well enough and strong enough to come home.

The only problem with her dreams for Little Rock, Tina learned early on in months of searching for answers, was that little information on the emotional aspects of blindness and raising a visually impaired child existed. The only information she could find was medical. Again, Tina was not put off and instead redoubled her quest.

She collected information from other parents and doctors, and chronicled her own experiences with Little Rock in the beginning as well as today. Her information became the foundation for the first Family Resource Center at Children's Hospital in Philadelphia, established so other parents of visually impaired children don't have to experience all the struggles and agonies Tina and Rocco Sr. did.

(continued)

Tina and Rocco Sr. took a hands-on development approach to raising Little Rock, and they worked hard so their family would be and is as normal as possible—only they talk a lot more, says Tina.

"Rocco Jr. is always a person first, and he is blind second. We never fell into the trap, 'Why me?'" says Tina. "The experience of having a blind child has made us who we are today. It gives us purpose and drives our every passion in life."

Today Tina lives and breathes her work with the Little Rock Foundation while raising Little Rock and running the Little Rock Camp, a summer camp she founded for visually impaired kids.

Meanwhile, Little Rock has embraced the joy of life to its fullest, too. He has mainstreamed into regular schools thanks to his parents' efforts to work with him. He's an accomplished musician, and he's an advocate for the blind and visually impaired. He's even testified before Congress and the New Jersey Legislature.

Little Rock isn't quite sure yet what's next—whether politics or music is his destiny. He's recorded a number of songs, and after testifying in front of the Legislature against cutting the budget for blind and visually impaired programs in New Jersey, that state's governor, Jon Corzine, named October Blindness Awareness Month!

From the depths of what could have been a trap of sadness and depression, Tina instead chose to embrace the joy of life and happiness, and she and her family thrive.

Listen to the "Voices"

"It feels good to take your own tragic experience and share it as a success," says Jenifer Westphal, 47, mother of three, including now-15-year-old son Kyle, who was diagnosed with autism in 1998. Jenifer and her husband, Jeffrey—like the Fiorentinos—were frustrated by the lack of information on their child's disability. Jenifer, like Tina, then a stay-at-home mom, decided to do something about it, and along with her husband founded the nonprofit Kyle's Treehouse to "empower everyone touched by autism to make effective choices."

It started as an information resource, and today has become a community with hundreds of thousands of visitors every year.

"Most mothers become who—or whatever—it takes to make a difference in their child's life. I wanted to do that in my whole life," says Jenifer. "The experience with my child has been an impetus to be the best I can be at anything."

After founding the Treehouse, Jenifer says, her family wasn't as supportive as she would have liked. Tensions persisted over the years about her role as a mother and a subject matter expert on autism. Jenifer says she felt unhappy and unsuccessful as a mother with an autistic child. But her success with Kyle—today he's an ordinary teen mainstreamed into regular schools—and the foundation have proved that her inner voice was right.

"I learned I could trust myself," Jennifer says. "My deeper unhappiness came from my [lack of] confidence. I have now found my voice—my own voice. . . . I'm happy to say I really took the time to be the best person I could be. . . . Mothers need to mother themselves."

Authentically Happy

Meet Kyle Westphal, 15, diagnosed with autism as a toddler. Today Kyle is a typical teenager with an extraordinary story that began as an infant and involved the determination and love of his parents to find the cause and the right treatment to help their child thrive.

As Kyle grew from an infant to a toddler, he changed from an outgoing and happy child to one who was very withdrawn. When Kyle was about 3, his parents, Jeff and Jenifer, became concerned. The two years that followed were a confusing and heart-wrenching period—not knowing what was wrong with Kyle until his diagnosis. After seeing numerous specialists and enduring a battery of tests, Kyle was diagnosed with autism in 1998.

The Westphals struggled but finally found a treatment for their son. After more than four years of therapy through

(continued)

The Son-Rise Program® at The Autism Treatment Center of America™, Kyle emerged from his autistic state.

It's a story of treatment success and a happy ending because of the optimism, strength, and perseverance of Kyle's parents, especially his mother.

Jenifer's story is one of triumph and success—success for thousands of other people, too. She, along with her husband, founded Kyle's Treehouse (a nonprofit information clearinghouse and community dedicated to helping families with autistic kids make the right decisions.

Doing Your Best

"We were put here with talents, and the extent to which we are utilizing them for a higher purpose makes us happy," says Pam, 57, now a successful executive coach. Pam grew up in a very traditional, working-class family that didn't believe girls needed to go to college. She went to work because she needed to support herself, and found work a blessing. "You are endowed with talents and are expected to use them to make the world a better place," she says.

Pam loved school and excelled in it, and that success propelled her forward. She put herself through college after putting her then-husband through school, too!

In addition to being a full-time executive, Pam was "full-time mom and full-time dad" to daughter, Katie, now 21. "Katie has learning disabilities, attention-deficit disorder, and obsessive-compulsive disorder . . . which went misdiagnosed for a long time," says Pam. "When she was in fifth grade, she was reading like a 4-year-old."

Katie's handicaps made raising her very challenging and time-consuming. Pam's parents would help out, but guilt was attached to the help. Pam says she constantly felt guilty even though she spent all her free time doing the very best she could for her daughter.

"Having a handicapped child and being a single mom was very difficult," she says. As a single mom (and even when she was married), Pam would work all day, get home from work and spend hours every night helping Katie with her homework.

During the seven years Pam was single, she says, she thought constantly of her daughter and made no time for herself. That was okay, though, says Pam. She did what she needed to do for her daughter. Work intruded on any private time, and even though she had a live-in nanny, that meant a 20-something person living in her house.

Through all the hardships and struggles, pangs of guilt, and doubt, Pam always embraced life as the "naturally happy" person she is. Her only regrets "I wish I had Katie in public schools; we would have taken a different tack and identified her issues earlier."

Pam says, too, that she should have had the confidence to move forward faster in her career. That would have allowed her to make a greater contribution.

Reclaiming Your Life

Our challenges and choices as working moms mold each of us into who we are. If we choose, as Pam did, to surrender all our personal time for our children, although it may feel right at the time, it may not be sustainable. In the long term, sacrificing all our personal time is not healthy for us as vibrant human beings. We lose the balance that centers us and grounds our families.

Happiness Tip: Knowing when to say "no" and how to do so without feeling guilty increases life satisfaction and, therefore, happiness.

The Power of "No"

Renee Peterson Trudeau, president of Career Strategists, life balance coach and author of *The Mother's Guide to Self-Renewal: How to Reclaim, Rejuvenate, and Rebalance Your Life* (Balanced Living Press, 2008), shares her Nine Creative Ways to Say No* (and reserve "yes" for what you really want to do):

1. **Just no:** "Thanks, I'll have to pass on that." (Say it, then stop talking.)
2. **The gracious no:** "I really appreciate you asking me, but my time is already committed."

3. **The "I'm sorry" no:** "I wish I could, but it's just not going to work right now."

4. **The "It's someone else's decision" no:** "I promised my coach (therapist, husband, etc.) I wouldn't take on any more projects right now. I'm working on creating more balance in my life."

5. **The "My family is the reason" no:** "Thanks so much for the invite, but that's the day of my son's soccer game, and I never miss those."

6. **The "I know someone else" no:** "I just don't have time right now. Let me recommend someone who may be able to help you."

7. **The "I'm already booked" no:** "I appreciate your thinking of me, but I'm afraid I'm already booked that day."

8. **The "Setting boundaries" no:** "Let me tell you what I can do . . . " Then limit the commitment to what will be comfortable for you.

9. **The "Not no, but not yes" no:** "Let me think about it, and I'll get back to you."

The next time you are ready to give up your 15 minutes of quiet time for your child, think about how you and your physical and emotional being set the tone and model the behavior for your family. Then ask yourself: Is this really necessary? Will I do more harm to my child if I say "yes" or if I say "no"? What we hope you see in these pages is that selflessly saying yes all the time can be more detrimental than if you take time you need as a working mother to reenergize, to breathe. That way, you're at your best for your children, your family, and your job no matter what external pressures and stresses come your way.

Strategies and Insights

Renee Trudeau shares her strategies and insights for balanced living[2]

♦ **Know your top priorities, and effectively manage your energy.** What in life is most important to you? How good are you at managing your energy? What is draining you? What is fueling you? Are you comfortable saying "no" and not over-extending yourself? Create an "absolute yes" list and adhere to it! *"Things which matter most should never be at the mercy of things which matter least." —Goethe*

◆ **Make your self-renewal a priority.** By filling your cup first, you'll have more to give to clients, family, and friends, you're able to function at your optimum, and you'll be setting an example for healthy, balanced living for those around you. Self-care (on all levels—physical, mental, emotional, spiritual) should be part of your everyday life.

◆ **Build a personal support system.** How much professional and personal support, and what kind, do you need to feel nurtured, emotionally healthy, and stress-free? Learn to ask for and receive help. Reevaluate your support needs every three months; these needs change based on your current life stage. *"Having a support system when going through a transition or challenging or stressful time can have a huge impact on how you experience the journey."—Renee Trudeau*

◆ **Be more present in all you do.** Stress and the feeling of being overwhelmed are often exacerbated by dwelling on the past or living in the future. By spending more time living in the present and focusing on what is most important in the here and now, the calmer and more effective we become. In general, we experience a greater sense of balance and integration when we live in the moment. One effective way to be more present is to be mindful about how and when we use technology (cell phones, e-mail, and so on).

Trudeau also suggests four areas of self-renewal that help us to reenergize and be at our best as mothers and in our jobs:

1. **Physical renewal:** Eat foods that are healthy and nourish your body; get enough sleep; make sure you're hydrated.
2. **Emotional renewal:** Create time for heart-to-heart talks with close friends or mentors; ditch self-criticism and judgmental thinking about your actions and thoughts.

3. **Spiritual renewal:** Take time to be alone and think or write, and connect with your authentic self; take a walk in a park or out in nature; meditate or pray.

4. **Mental/intellectual renewal:** Read a good book or enhance your knowledge about an area that interests you; challenge yourself by signing up for a class, group, or workshop and learn something new.

Authentically Happy

Carmela, now 46, was 14 when she met Sal and married by the time she was 19. Their first child, Dawn, was born soon after. Five years later her second daughter, Mia, arrived. Carmela was a dedicated mother and wife just as her husband wanted it for many years.

After about 10 years, Carmela decided to fulfill a dream and go back to school to become a medical assistant. After nine months of full-time schooling, on the date she was to graduate, her daughter was institutionalized at a drug addiction center. It took Dawn only nine months without daily supervision to drive her health into the ground and her mother to tears with blame for her selfish desire to want a career in addition to being a wife and mother.

Carmela never followed her dream because she was faced with the treatment and custody needs of her daughters. Her husband wasn't supportive, and eventually they separated. Sal took custody of the children, and Carmela was left on her own for the first time since she was 14 years old.

At first, Carmela was devastated and wound up hospitalized after an accidental overdose of prescription medication for an ongoing medical condition and depression. But she chose to do more than just overcome her depression or simply survive. She chose to thrive.

Against overwhelming odds, Carmela pulled her life together and started a business cleaning homes and doctors' offices. By

2003, she was stable, on her own, and financially sound. Now, five years later, she has a full book of business with clients who love her, and her daughters are both happy and healthy.

Carmela is in a relationship, and looks back on her journey with appreciation for the opportunities she has found to be happy. She says it's not the story she imagined as a young girl. But she admits it's the happily ever after that fits her best. And, she says, "Elbow grease goes a long way."

Coping with Divorce

Divorce, no matter its circumstances, tears at your emotions. Often we underestimate how powerful those emotions are. Taking care of yourself physically and emotionally is essential to manage the trauma of divorce. It also is important to understand that it is both healthy and normal to grieve your divorce.

Let's consider some coping strategies to help you get through the emotional turmoil of divorce and move on to creating a better life post-divorce.

Some thoughts to keep in mind:

- ◆ Keep the cost of your divorce down by using your time and the right resources wisely. If you're overwrought, don't pay your attorney to listen to something that would be better heard by a therapist who specializes in divorces and can truly offer ways to help you cope.
- ◆ You're resilient so don't dwell on your despair. Even if you wanted out of a marriage, mourning its death is all part of the recovery process. Your level of happiness likely will return to its set point or normal level. You will recover.

For more helpful information on how to deal with divorce, check out Deborah Moskovitch's *The Smart Divorce: Proven Strategies and Valuable Advice from 100 Top Divorce Lawyers, Financial Advisers, Counselors, and Other Experts* (Chicago Review Press, 2007).

Costly Lessons

"When I was going through my own divorce, it was important for me to realize the costs associated with sharing my concerns with the people I had hired to help me. I once received a bill from my attorney for an hour of 'emotional venting.' I guess I thought that was included in his fee. Listening to me as a client is important, but I still had to pay for it.

"After that, I was more careful about getting into an emotional conversation with my legal team. That sort of conversation is better shared with a divorce therapist. The legal team was better prepared to focus on the details of the divorce settlement that they could help me influence—things like custody issues and moving costs. Recognizing the delineation of responsibilities and areas of expertise helps anyone going through her divorce better maintain her well-being and budget. Getting unexpected bills, after all, stresses us even more.

"With this in mind, carefully think about what you truly need to discuss with each of the advisors on your divorce team, including the legal team, your therapist, or personal coach, and your financial advisor (if you have the luxury of having different individuals involved in the decision-making). Make a list of the topics you need to discuss and then make sure each is directed to the right person before you get a bill for an hour of expert time you didn't expect."

—Cathy Greenberg (happy, divorced, working mother in a new long-term relationship)

Take Care of Yourself Emotionally

When we go through a divorce, everyone in our lives experiences our emotional ups and downs. The circle of pain can be overwhelming. A good therapist may help by listening without judgment. But the real answers are always the answers that are right for you at work or at home.

A Mother's Story

During a divorce, it's essential to take care of yourself physically and emotionally. I found that out the hard way.
—Cathy Greenberg

"When I went through my divorce, as a working mother I did not have the luxury of hiding in my comfy pajamas with a box of chocolates as I had envisioned from watching soap operas as a child. I still had to get up, go to work, pay the bills, and take care of my daughter.

"By all outward indications, my life as a single working mother was a success. But on the inside, my unhappy state of affairs ravaged my body physically. Sometimes I just went numb. It was easier that way. In the end my body was smarter than I was, and this lack of attention to my needs caught up with me. My denial found its way into my lymph nodes, my reproductive organs, and almost destroyed my immune system. Taking care of myself by taking care of business was not the answer. A few short years after my divorce, it almost killed me.

"Faced with the truth about my health, I couldn't ignore my desire for true happiness. It was clear that my happiness needed to come first, or there would be no one to take care of my young daughter and no job to help me support myself or my true happiness."

Self-help has its upside—you can take it or leave it. Getting the right support means facing up to the reality of what you can handle and finding the support you really need to get a handle on your life. To help you learn what happiness means to you and to get a better handle on achieving your own success, try these tips to give yourself a break:

- Evaluate other times of crisis in your life. What did you do to get through those times? Perhaps some of the coping strategies you used then could be useful now.
- Try to visualize how you would like your life to look post-divorce. Ask yourself what you need to do to develop that

fulfilling life. Start doing those things now. Being proactive will make you feel better.

◆ Take care of yourself physically and emotionally to help lessen the stress. That means take time for yourself, too.

◆ Don't overlook your children's physical and emotional health, either. It's easy to do when you're overwrought yourself.

Checklist for Working Mothers Going through Divorce

◆ Find your support network—friends, relatives, support groups, clergy.

◆ Take care of yourself emotionally.

◆ Don't be a martyr; take some time for yourself.

◆ Talk to your boss at work, if possible, to let him/her know about your divorce, as the emotional aspects can affect your performance in the workplace.

◆ Make time for yourself.

◆ Eat healthily, stay fit; you'll feel better.

Source: Deborah Moskovitch, author of *The Smart Divorce: Proven Strategies and Valuable Advice from 100 Top Divorce Lawyers, Financial Advisers, Counselors, and Other Experts* (Chicago Review Press, 2007).

Bottom Lines: Exercises to Try

DISCOVERING AND CELEBRATING LIFE'S LITTLE MIRACLES AND SMALL VICTORIES
This exercise will help you understand the function, nature, and implications of your emotions.

1. Start by identifying as many little miracles as you can. To help you, think in terms of:
   ◆ Your body/physiology (e.g., Your body manages your physiology with attention from you. Your heart knows to beat, your lungs breathe air without your attention to

---

your organs. Many small miracles make up the human body without your immediate action.)

- ◆ Cognitive/emotional (e.g., Cognitive/emotional responses to seeing pictures or experiencing nature evoke heartfelt memories or feelings with little management on our part.)
- ◆ Spiritual (e.g., Spiritual feelings can come from an infinite number of daily or weekly experiences which help us feel connected to our roles as mothers, women, people, and to our humanity.)
- ◆ Other

2. Now concentrate on small victories. These are what you have achieved or accomplished. To help you get started, think in terms of:
   - ◆ Your sense of purpose
   - ◆ Your health
   - ◆ Your relationships (start with the relationship you have with yourself)

3. Now that you've completed steps 1 and 2, answer the following questions:
   - ◆ What do you feel at this very moment?
   - ◆ On a scale of 1–10, with 1 being very low and 10 very strong, how would you rate your energy?
   - ◆ How would you characterize your sense of well-being right now?

4. What would happen to the quality of your life if you were to consciously take note of the little miracles and small victories that are all around you every day of your life?

Chapter 8

Pulling It All Together

*At any given moment, we are not firing on all cylinders, so
we need a well-rounded way of life and people in it to
help us be our best.*

—Benita Fitzgerald Mosley, mother, executive, Olympic athlete

Working moms frequently feel that they live two lives–at home as a
mother and partner, and at work as a colleague. Often, they describe
themselves as different people at home and at work. We all adapt to
the role we're playing at the moment, but our values shouldn't have to
change between home and work. Neither should we have to forget
what we learn from our kids the minute we walk into work, or forget
what we know at work as soon as we walk into our homes.

The happiest people are those who feel integrated—their work
and their personal lives are separate but connected by a common
thread of values and priorities.

What do you love about you? Ignore everyone else's opinion, and
focus only on your opinion of yourself. What are the best parts of you?
When are you most at peace?

No matter how hectic your life, your answers to these questions
matter. They are the essence of happiness for you. The authentic you
may be buried beneath layers of responsibilities, but uncovering it
remains the central part of your true happiness. All these things
complete us.

A former boss called these people "SWANs"—Smart, Works Hard,
and Nice! Many SWANs are working mothers who truly live an

integrated life, and as a result, get high marks both at work and at home.

Focusing on Your Authentic Life

We work hard and we do a good job. Our companies promote us to where they need us, but not necessarily to where we want to be. Years into a career or a job, we may find ourselves far from what we truly like or once liked to do. Having a child helps us refocus on who we are because it leads us to think about our values as we try to bring our best self to our children.

Living your values models the behavior most of us hope our children will follow. Seek work that allows you to live your authentic life. That may not mean you need a new job. It could be that you simply need to adjust the job you have now. Trust your instincts and see the world as full of possibilities. You have more control over your life than you think. You can become more adaptable and able to flourish in an unpredictable and ever-changing world when you take the time to use your whole brain.

By applying our whole brain function as discussed earlier, our decisions are made with more highly developed areas of the brain. This means our decision-making skills move from the reptilian (the survival brain) to the executive brain (the more social brain). Ultimately, practice using the higher-order functioning systems in the brain results in more integrated decision-making that can lead to a greater capacity to influence our lives. Using your whole brain to think through the many ways you can influence your life leads to a more integrated way of being. The overall result provides a deeper sense of accomplishment and ultimately a happier you.

Know Yourself

Olympic gold medalist Benita Fitzgerald Mosley embraces life's possibilities in the many roles she plays—mother, daughter, wife, athlete, career woman, community member—and she thrives. At the beginning of this book, she spoke of how her many different experiences growing up and as an adult enhance who she is and what she does—whether in the boardroom, the home, or the community.

"I started running track at age 12 and played the flute as well. I had poor self-esteem as a child," Mosley says. "I did not think I was cute until I was more accomplished in school and on the track team. In sixth and seventh grade when I ran track and won races, I felt really good about myself. This helped me overcome [my weaknesses] and apply my strengths and talents.

"I think we all really need family time and community activities that help us lead well-rounded lives," Mosley adds. "At any given moment, we are not firing on all cylinders, so we need a well-rounded way of life and people in it to help us be our best—coaches, teachers, and family."

Like Mosley, you can develop your own well-rounded life by embracing all that's possible in your life. It starts with realizing that the choice of happiness—and job—is yours.

Think back to a time when you truly were being yourself, before the layers of responsibilities and external distractions piled up, and when you were appreciated for who you are. Think of a moment when you felt fully in the moment, strong, and valued. What were you doing? How were you doing it? How did you feel? Now ask yourself what this tells you about who you are. Take a few minutes to really revel in the thoughts and the feelings. And then, think about what it would take to feel that way again. Open your thoughts and your mind, and embrace the possibilities.

Authentically Happy

Working mothers and authors, Cathy Greenberg and Barrett Avigdor, recall a moment in each of their lives when they were truly being and feeling who they are, and what that moment and those feelings reveal about each of them:

Cathy: I was 18 years old. I was wearing khaki shorts and observing a group of monkeys on the island of Bermuda. I was great at observing animal behavior—seeing patterns,

(continued)

recognizing shifts in the group, predicting behavior. I was good at it, and I loved it.

I still love observing behavior in people and drawing conclusions that help people enhance their effectiveness and happiness.

Barrett: I was 19 and working for the summer as an interpreter at a Cuban refugee center in Fort McCoy, Wisconsin. I spent long and exhilarating days helping Cuban refugees to find their relatives in the United States. I felt useful and important.

I love using my unique set of skills to help people. I like being useful, particularly to people who truly want and need my help.

Avoiding the Detours

Living our values is not always easy. The quest for money, power, and status can dissuade us and derail us from our journey. For most of us, money, power, and status do not bring happiness. They help us to look successful in the eyes of others but rarely bring happiness. Becoming self-aware, articulating your values, and then aligning your time and energy to those values brings self-trust and spontaneity that will lead to greater self-trust and lasting happiness.

Happiness Tip: You may take a different path than the one you envisioned, but the detours are worth it because you learn more from your failures than your successes.

Sometimes, we get in our own way and block our own happiness. We face internal and external barriers, too, those negative voices that create self-doubt and cause us to pause instead of move forward. Some of those voices may say:

- ◆ I'm not good enough to take this role.
- ◆ I'm too old to learn a new skill.

◆ I'd love to do that but I don't have time.
◆ If I don't take care of things at home, they won't get done.

Self-Coaching Break: Taking the Bait

We are strong, and we can overcome the negative with our positive and with our appreciation of all that we have, which is at the core of our happiness. Instead of choosing to accept the negative voices, we can learn to coach ourselves into embracing the mentality of abundance; that we as working mothers can happily achieve whatever it is that brings us joy both at home with our children and families, and in our careers.

If you want to change the negative sound track that keeps running in your head, you may need to write a new script for those voices. It may feel strange at first but, with time, those positive voices will become as much as part of you as the negative voices have been. Here are some ideas for your new script. Feel free to add you own:

◆ I can do this.
◆ Asking for help is smart; it is not a sign of weakness.
◆ In the scheme of things, this is not such a big deal.
◆ I am being true to my values.
◆ My intuition is a positive force for good decision-making.
◆ I will listen to others but make up my own mind.
◆ I have good judgment.

Working Mothers' Advice for Others

In a focus group of working mothers at a major mid-Atlantic regional bank, participants offered the following advice to other working mothers:

◆ "You are not Superwoman, and it's okay if you can't do it all."
◆ "Do what you enjoy, not what people expect of you."

- ◆ "Don't feel you need to justify your decisions."
- ◆ "Stay positive, be organized, and understand the needs and responsibilities of work and how to balance them with family."
- ◆ "Plan for everything, but allow for the unexpected."
- ◆ "You can have it all, just maybe not all the time."
- ◆ "Balance is key, as is a love of what you do."
- ◆ "Don't expect to do everything to perfection. What you can do is good enough."
- ◆ "It is possible to be happy in both realms—work and family, it's your choice."
- ◆ "Do a little laundry every night, it gives you more freedom on weekends."
- ◆ "Be nice to yourself."
- ◆ "'Compromise' is the key word to remember."
- ◆ "Put your family first, but not to the point where you jeopardize your job."

"The key to psychological well-being is learning what you're doing that feeds the reflexive habits of insecurity (worry, doubts, fears, and negatives) and what you can do to starve these habits," says Joseph J. Luciani, Ph.D. of Cresskill, N.J., a clinical psychologist and author of the best-selling *Self-Coaching* series. He advocates self-coaching as a way to help ourselves. "As I see it, positive thinking and positive affirmations are only 50 percent of the equation. The other 50 percent has to do with positively believing what you tell yourself. Bottom line, if you aren't able to embrace and live what you're telling yourself, there will be no change."[1]

Capitalize on Your Leadership Skills

"Any experience where you have to provide direction and make things happen—whether it's as a Girl Scout troop leader or the CEO—is leadership," says Jill Smart, working mother of two kids, 16 and 11, and chief human resources officer for Accenture.

Mothering is leadership training that makes us better at our jobs, and our jobs make us better at mothering, agreed almost all the mothers we interviewed. Integrating the two aspects of our lives makes us better at whatever we do.

Work and Home in Tandem

Motherhood and work are not an either/or proposition. "It's mutually enriching," says author Jamie Woolf. When she became a mom 14 years ago, Woolf says, she saw the crossover between the skills of a good mom and those of a good leader. "Our goal as parents is to capture the full potential of our kids. At work we seek to capture the full potential of our employees."

> *Being a mother has made me a better human being.*
> —Pam, executive coach, mother of one (a special-needs child),
> and stepmother of two

"Learning what it takes to be a leader has helped me be a better mother," says Nancy Laben, deputy general counsel for Accenture. "A good mother is someone who prepares her kids to do better than she has done in the world—better in terms of achievement and in doing good; showing them how to be self-sufficient, kind, being the best person they can be, and learning how to be happy.

"A good mother knows she is not responsible for her children's happiness," Laben adds.

As we mentioned earlier, virtually every mother we interviewed said that being a mother made her better at her job. Those same women said they use some of the skills and techniques they learn at work to make them better mothers.

That crossover of skills makes us better in whatever we do. For Smart, her work has "completely and totally" influenced the way she parents. "The organizational skill it takes to be successful at Accenture helps a lot with my kids. The success I've achieved through my hard work has been noticed by my 16-year-old daughter. It shows her that hard work can make up for a lot of things— you can overcome initial failure if you ask for help and work hard. . . . I ask for help a lot at work, and I've taught my kids that asking for help does not make you weak or a failure. Also, I've learned at work that if I overreact, it has a big negative impact on people, so I try not to overreact at home."

At work, Smart says, she's changed, too. "My style has changed. I've learned about priorities; what's worth getting riled up about and what is not. I've learned not to sweat the small stuff. I've learned to be more patient. I think I've also become more open-minded to other people's ideas. When my kids got older and I started learning from them, I became more open. I think I respect the work-life balance of others more."

Mothers learn to multitask, but that's a mixed blessing, says Victoria, a physician and mother of three. "Multitasking makes you productive but does not allow you to be [fully] in the present moment. But the ability to juggle many things makes you resourceful."

Conversely, Victoria says, her work has taught her to be calm in the face of crisis and to hone her skills as a communicator—both attributes that have helped her as a mother.

Says Babette, a working mother in Paris, France: "I've learned a lot about my strengths and shortcomings as a mother. I've learned fortitude and balance. I've learned what is and is not happiness. I've learned what makes a relationship work and how my actions impact others."

A Mother's Story

Dee Dee Myers, working mother, author, and former press secretary for President Bill Clinton, talks about how motherhood has changed her work:

"Changes are gradual but, looking back over almost nine years now, I am more focused, more efficient. What did I do with all my free time before I had kids?

"I work at home now, which is mostly a blessing. I'm better at getting to win/win. I did not appreciate before how important it is for everyone to be happy. I realize now it's important for people to feel they've been heard. I'm better at setting boundaries.

"My worldview has changed somewhat, too. I always thought it was important for women to be involved in all aspects of public life. I feel that way even more now. I see the world as more dangerous than I did before. Having kids makes you more sensitive to specific and abstract dangers.

"I have a broader view of what it means to have meaningful work. I realize how things close to home—volunteering at school or being a stay-at-home parent—can be very valuable and meaningful.

"No one answer works for everyone, and I appreciate more now the importance of options for women. You need to listen to your internal voice and do what feels right for you."

More mothers single out the lessons they've learned as mothers that transfer to the workplace and beyond:

◆ "As a mom, you learn what matters. You learn resilience. Being a mom teaches you to be calm. The stakes could not be higher when you're a mom, so it teaches you to handle tough situations. Being a mom gives you a calm perspective."—Flavia, mother of two, Buenos Aires, Argentina

◆ "I've learned that you need to explain clearly your expectations, to be patient, to be more sensitive to others' capabilities and limitations. Being a mother has taught me that everyone is different."—Claire, mother of three, Los Angeles

◆ "Having my daughter made me much less egotistical. You are no longer the center of your world."—Cynthia, mother of one, Amsterdam, The Netherlands

Roadblocks to Leadership at Home

Being effective at work can transition to success at home if we allow ourselves the freedom to let that happen. Not all successful working mothers transfer their workplace leadership skills to mothering, though.

Many moms, according to author Woolf, say, "I don't want to think about leadership when I'm home." In her research for her book, Woolf says she was surprised that many very successful businesswomen felt incompetent at home. Because motherhood is so emotionally charged and important, people forget to use their executive skills, she adds.

Life has a way of not always turning out the way we dreamed or even planned. "I studied to be a nurse, but I wasn't prepared to be a mom," says mother of three and clinical nurse specialist Jill. "Motherhood is hard, and no one gets training. I'm not all that different as a mom than my mom, except my mom didn't work when we were little."

Heather, working mother of three, says she "never imagined the trade-offs" necessary as a working mother. It's hard to make everything work, she says, but with her sense of fulfillment and strong support from her husband and three children, she has found the right balance.

Leadership Style

Seeing yourself as a leader elevates you above the drudgery to find the joy and the importance of motherhood, says Woolf. In *Mom-in-Chief*, she helps each of us understand the connection between leadership at work and how to bring it home to help us fulfill our parenting potential and gracefully navigate parenting challenges. Some leadership strategies that translate from workplace to home, says Woolf, include:

- ◆ Setting big-picture goals.
- ◆ Discovering your own leadership style.
- ◆ Managing conflict.
- ◆ Understanding family culture.
- ◆ Leading through crisis.

◆ Navigating the growing pains of your children's adolescence.
◆ Balancing priorities.

Your parenting style is your approach to being a parent and the default mode you lapse into in crisis. It's also the biggest source of conflict between moms and dads. By being aware of our leadership style, we can be more effective, especially during times of crisis, and not overplay our natural tendencies, Woolf adds. (To learn more about *Mom-in-Chief* and what Woolf says about parenting leadership styles, visit her web site (http://blog.mominchief.com/2009/01/).

> *By looking at yourself as a leader, it elevates you above the drudgery to see the joy and the importance of motherhood.*
> —Jamie Woolf, author of *Mom-in-Chief*

Authenticity

You are the same person at home as at work. Your style of leadership, whether as CEO of your family or in the workplace, is basically the same. You will be your most effective if you work with your authentic style. The more authentic you are, the more active you will be. The more active you are, the happier you will be, says Woolf. Being authentic means working to your strengths and aligning your priorities to your values. You can still change and grow as a leader. Everyone— children, and employees —reacts favorably to authenticity.

For example, if your strength is diving deeply into one project at a time and you don't like to multitask, talk with your family about how each member can take on responsibilities so you don't have to organize everything. If you are the type of leader at work who likes to empower others to grow and stretch, do the same for your kids.

Focus on Your Strengths

To maximize your success and minimize your stress, play to your strengths—those abilities you considered at the beginning of this chapter when we asked what you think you're good at.

Be Your Best

All of us become more productive, more creative, and less stressed human beings if we find ways to play to our strengths most of the time. Marcus Buckingham has published several books (including *The Truth About You*, and *Go, Put Your Strengths to Work*) based on his work with The Gallup Organization consulting with companies to determine what makes great teams great. His research has shown that the best teams, those that consistently outperform their competition, are those in which each member uses his or her strengths most of the time. Strengths, in this context, are those activities you love to do and are good at doing. If you are good at something but it drains you, it's not a strength but a weakness.

The same holds true at home.

Take the Strength-Based Approach

Developing our strengths helps us to become better and more adept at using those strengths; our self-confidence and happiness gets a boost, and that wears off on those around us at home and at work.

Stress Reducer

This strengths-based approach is especially valuable for working moms because our time is at a premium. We need to have the biggest positive impact we can in the time we have available to work, and the best way to do that is to focus on our strengths. The approach also has the added benefit of reducing stress. When working moms are less stressed at work, we can be better moms at home.

The kids we talked to wholeheartedly agree. Annie, 10, knows the difference between when her mom has had a good day at work and when she's had a bad day. "When Mom has a good day at work, she comes home in a good mood, makes a good dinner, and usually helps me with homework or plays a game with me. When she has a bad day, it seems like I get on her nerves no matter what I do."

Don't Ignore Weaknesses, Work Around Them

It's a myth that you can turn a weakness into a strength if you just work hard enough. You can't. Many of us strive to be perfect in everything. We minimize our strengths and focus intently on our weaknesses in an effort to become excellent at all aspects of our work. If we define weaknesses, as Buckingham does, as those things that drain your energy, then the more you work on them the more they drain you. When you are drained at work, you can't be your best at home or at work.

Focusing on your weaknesses also can create physical problems that can manifest themselves as health issues like aches, pains, colds, and weight gain or loss. We don't want to avoid weaknesses. Instead, we need to understand our weaknesses and develop strategies for working around them.

When you feel your weaknesses catching up to you at home or in the workplace, reflect and regroup. Is there a way for you to do what needs to be done by relying on your strengths? If not, can you team up with someone who complements your weakness with strength? This may even be a way to empower your children to step up and offer their strengths.

A Mother's Story

I love to entertain, but cooking for a lot of people is very stressful for me. The solution, it turns out, was in my family.
—Barrett Avigdor

"For years, I would have people for dinner at least once a week because I love having long and lively conversations with a variety of friends. After awhile, the work of designing a menu, shopping, and cooking started to slow me down.

"When my son turned 15, he discovered that he loves to cook. For him, the more complicated the menu and the bigger the party, the better. His younger brother likes to make the dessert and to help serve the meal.

"Now, he does all my cooking for dinner parties. He loves the opportunity to show off, and I love the opportunity to spend time with my friends and enjoy a great meal that I didn't cook."

To help you better understand your strengths and weaknesses, focus for a few minutes on both, and ask yourself the following questions:

◆ Think about the last time you were so engrossed in what you were doing that time flew by. What were you doing? Try to think of a few examples. These are strengths.

◆ Now think of activities that you dread doing. When you do those activities, time drags. These are your weaknesses.

◆ Make a list of strengths and weaknesses. Each week, try to spend a few more minutes working to your strengths and fewer minutes on your weaknesses.

Your Motivations and Success

Once you have a basic understanding of your strengths, you can learn to recognize what motivates you and apply those strengths to achieve the goals you set for yourself. Motivations are those qualities that help to drive your success. Some people are motivated by achievement, some by power or control, some by access to others or affiliations they gain, and others are motivated by harmony and belonging. Understanding how you're motivated will help you build on who you already are. There are numerous books and web sites that offer assessment tools, many of which are free. We've listed a number of them in the Additional Resources section at the back of the book.

When you come to understand your strengths and motivations, you can present your most positive self. This is the part of you that others find the most appealing, the part that will be the best at work and at home. Your authentic self is your best self. Let your authentic self come out every day—at home and at work.

Bottom Lines: Exercises to Try

ADAPTABILITY DIARY

Increase your ability to adapt at home and at work.

Take inventory daily for one week and capture your responses using the two categories: home and work. Using this chart, create a

---

Figure 8.1   Adaptation Exercise

EVENT	Day	Home	Work
Situation			
Response			
Worked Better			
Next Time			
Notes			

daily inventory for each day of the week starting with Sunday and continuing through each day until you have one full week of charts to review. (See Figure 8.1.)

- ◆ List your answers with honesty—not the way you would like them to be.
  - ■ First row is: What was the unexpected situation?
  - ■ Second row is: How did you respond?
  - ■ Third row is: What might have worked better?
  - ■ Fourth row is: What steps can I take to be better prepared next time?
- ◆ List things that occurred in your day that were not expected at home. Examples may include:
  - ■ Child has a fever
  - ■ Babysitter is sick
  - ■ Alarm clock did not go off
  - ■ Flat tire or other car trouble
- ◆ List the responses you had to that situation.
  - ■ What may have worked better or what were you most proud of as you review your response?
  - ■ Next time, what will you do?
- ◆ List things that occurred in your day that you did not expect at work. Examples may include:

(continued)

- Unscheduled meetings.
- Urgent project assignment.
- Angry customer.
- Missed lunch.

◆ List the responses you had to that situation.
  - What may have worked better or what were you most proud of as you review your response?
  - Next time, what will you do?

Applying Your Strength to Adapt

◆ Review your week—look for patterns at work and at home.

◆ What responses are you most proud of?
  - How did your response improve your outcome/ situation?
  - How would you build on that response in the future?

◆ How easy was it for you to think of ways you could have responded even better, once the situation was resolved? (Isn't it funny, how we can resolve problems more positively when we are not in the middle of the situation?)

Chapter 9

Happily Ever After—Your Story

You don't find happiness—you release it.
—Joseph J. Luciani, Ph.D., clinical psychologist and author
of the best-selling *Self-Coaching* series

If we follow our dreams, pursue our goals, live our values, and love ourselves as we are, everyone wins. Our children and families win because we are happier and less stressed, our fellow workers and our companies win because we are more productive and creative. When you are happy, you are the best version of you. Happiness is the tide that lifts all the boats in your life.

In these pages we hope we've helped you understand that happiness can be your reality. When you see and appreciate the abundance and joy of life, you will feel the positive impact in your life as a mother, in your career or job, and in your relationships. Happiness in within your grasp. Choose to reach for it, every day.

Authentically Happy: A Son's Story

Doug Barry published his first book, Wisdom for a Young CEO, *at the age of 15. His mother is a financial services executive.*

Doug Barry recounts a telling story of his working mother and how she steered her course so that work and family created a gratifying and satisfying mix for herself and for her kids.

(continued)

"When the lease was up on my mother's first luxury vehicle, a 1986 burger-brown BMW, a car she adored, she took my hand and led me out to the front steps of our house to watch one of the first material fruits of her professional success roll backward out of the driveway.

"'Wave good-bye, Dougie,' she said. It never impressed me that we were saying good-bye to anything other than an old object that had outlived its purpose, and I could hardly believe the sentimentality she infused into every retelling of the event.

"With the clarity of hindsight, I realize that she was beginning to peek her head through the clouds of corporate management and, at this momentous juncture, was more than likely looking back on the years of hard work that opened these more lucrative doors.

"After a recent dinner table conversation during which she told the story of our farewell to the old sedan with misty eyes, I asked her why she still thought so fondly of that car. She answered deliberately, as if all these years she had been telling me a fable hoping to prompt this very question.

"'It's important,' she said, 'when you achieve your goals and reach a destination, to remember how you got there. That car helped ferry me into a new phase of my career and it was the first you had ever ridden in.'

"My mother had, by the time the BMW left, achieved a balance between professional and personal life which I have always wished for in my own endeavors. She was there for us on every snow day, and shaved a few hours off of weekdays to see how a school project turned out. Work was always taken seriously, but when it was over, she was all ours. Though she enjoys the perks of a robust career, she was never eager to shed the worn-in clothes of her former positions and jump into the sleek new styles without first pausing in front of the mirror for one last look to acknowledge the places she had come from and the determination it took to move herself forward."

Happiness Is a Choice

We all meet obstacles in our journeys to happiness. Our focus sometimes drifts so that we end up reacting to problems instead of making the choice to proactively approach difficulties to find the solutions. We allow fear to hold us back and block our natural ability to engage our happiness factors.

Society sometimes compartmentalizes us as well, chastises us for working instead of staying home with the kids, and blames us for hurting our kids. Yet many working mothers—and their kids— have told you their happy stories. These are about happy working mothers who have recognized their strengths, embraced their joys, and triumphed. Their kids have thrived, too. The key is to find what makes you happy—whether it's working or staying at home—and do that. These women are happy in their jobs; they're happy in their home lives; and their children and families thrive, too. Their lives are not perfect. They have disappointments and setbacks like anyone else. The difference between these women and their un- happy counterparts is that happy working mothers choose to focus on the positives in their lives. They don't ignore the negatives—they change them if they can, and, if they cannot change them, they minimize them.

> *Nothing is 100 percent right or wrong. Don't strive for perfection. As long as you're doing the best you can, you're probably doing well.*
> —Susan, pharmacist and mother of four now-grown kids

Living in Two Worlds

From the time we're small, we dream of what we would like our lives to be, of where we want to go, what we'd like to do, and how we'll achieve those goals. We dream of careers, families, education, and status. Some of us dream of making a difference, helping others, and even changing the world. These dreams are a part of who we are. As working mothers, those dreams and aspirations often lie buried beneath responsibilities and struggles, submerged in obligations and other peoples' needs. Each of us has the choice to reawaken the possibilities. Start with happiness.

Your life today may be exactly as you envisioned it or nothing at all like you imagined it in your dreams of years ago. Either way, happiness is within the grasp of each of us if we learn to love ourselves, appreciate the beauty of life around us, and use our strengths to make our mark on the world.

Working mothers live in two separate spheres. With a mentality of abundance, you'll see that what you learn at work makes you a better mother and what you learn as a mother makes you better at your work. Each enhances the other. Working mothers with tenacity, skills, and leadership qualities thrive in what innovative business thinker, strategist, and author Gary Hamel refers to as the revolution of the new economy, the evolving workplace of the twenty-first century.

We are leaders trained in the trenches of motherhood. When the going gets tough, we know how to get support, to draw on our inner strength, and triumph. Our kids love us and are proud of us; our husbands, partners, and/or families love us, and are proud of us, too. Our happiness in part is about being proud of ourselves, what we do, and how we do it.

Overcoming the Fears

We've talked about our fears as working mothers, and how they can paralyze us into inaction at home and in the workplace and block our happiness if we choose to let them. Take a minute again to consider what some of those fears are that are blocking your happiness. After all, remember that naming the fear is the first step to overcoming it:

- ◆ Fear of having enough.
- ◆ Fear of being enough.
- ◆ Fear of learning new things.
- ◆ Fear of performance reviews.
- ◆ Fear of success.
- ◆ Fear of taking control.
- ◆ Fear of being very powerful.

Making the Workplace Family-Friendly

We all, men and women, want to raise happy children, keep families together, and lead fulfilling lives. We have an opportunity to create workplace policies that allow working parents—fathers and mothers—to balance their careers with their parental obligations. We need to support those parents who choose to stay home full time to care for their children—fathers as well as mothers—and make it easier for them to reenter the workforce if and when they're ready to do so. As parents, we shouldn't have to worry about losing our jobs or fret about the ridicule of fellow workers because of our chosen lifestyle.

The Virtual Office

Today's techno-savvy workplace is very different from that of our parents. In many jobs, it's possible to work remotely, and in today's economic environment, many companies embrace that option. Some companies have gone virtual, which means your workplace can be anywhere, and telecommuting at least occasionally has become a norm rather than an exception. These options open new doors for parents wanting to spend more time with our kids and families. That 24/7 work-style/lifestyle has a downside, too. It can rob us of our personal time if we allow it to. As with raising our kids, it's important that we set boundaries for our work time, work space, and personal needs.

A Mother's Story

Coauthor Cathy Greenberg personally experienced firsthand the downside of today's 24/7 work-style/lifestyle.

"I've chosen to make my life's work helping others avoid the pitfalls of circling the career track (one of six happiness traps outlined in *What Happy Women Know*, a book I coauthored with Dan Baker, Rodale Press).

"Through my executive coaching and leadership development consultancy at h2c, Happy Companies Healthy People, I have opened the door for both men and women to truly find their happiness at work and at home."

"The industrial world of work has vanished," says Sally Helgesen, leadership development consultant, coach, and author of several books, including *Thriving 24/7: Six Strategies for Taming the New World of Work* (Free Press, 2007). "Yet most of us are still trying to live by its obsolete rules. . . . We struggle to work harder, faster, and smarter, to discipline ourselves not to waste our moments, to multitask in order to keep up. Yet our heroic efforts often have the effect of robbing us of spontaneity and joy, making even pleasures that should refresh us feel like items on an endless to-do list that threatens to swallow us up."

What Working Moms Want

Working mothers want workplaces that recognize their second jobs as moms. In some places, such awareness exists—employers are open and understanding of special issues working mothers face. In others, employers are less understanding, and if a working mother takes time away from her job, the guilt creeps into the fabric of her relationships with her peers.

Consider a few more results from the Working Mother Media survey mentioned in Chapter 1[1]:

- 75 percent of working moms feel their bosses *are* supportive of their family needs.
- 69 percent had asked for changes at work.
- 74 percent got the changes they requested (most for more flexibility).

Rivalries and Roles

The recent history of working mothers in the United States is a complicated one. Thanks to the feminist movement, the doors of many professions and traditionally male jobs opened to women in the 1970s. Those pioneers felt they had to make the choice between marriage and career, so relatively few became working mothers.

By the 1980s, however, many young women felt emboldened enough to "have it all," so they started families while still pursuing careers. That is when we began to see the double standard. Men who worked to support their families were good providers. Women who did the same were selfish. Articles and reports created the false impression that the children of working mothers suffered as a result of the mothers being at work.

Rather than cast the stay-at-home-versus-go-to-work choice as something that each woman weighs for herself based on where she is happier, society decided to elevate the stay-at-home mom at the expense of the working mom. This overly simplified and judgmental view does a disservice to both men and women. The reality is that for both men and women, ambition can change over time as priorities in life change.

We are advocates for happiness. The best answer for working family members is for employers to give all their employees, men and women, the flexibility to mold their careers around their changing priorities. Working mothers are at the forefront, demanding more flexibility and, when they are in leadership positions, creating that flexibility for themselves and others. But if we truly want to change the workplace, men as well as women need to avail themselves of flexible schedules, sabbaticals, leaves, and other innovations of the twenty-first century workplace.

Your Happiness in Review

At the beginning of this book, we asked about the foundation of your happiness. We asked you to ask yourself what you need to do to be happy, what people play essential roles in your happiness, who or what is missing and why, and what it would take for you to achieve your true happiness.

Perhaps in the beginning—before you truly understood the importance of believing in yourself, living your values, and recognizing all the abundance in your life—those answers weren't as clear to you.

Below is another look at the ground rules for your happiness. Try asking yourself the questions again, with the emphasis on self-value and the joys in your life:

- ◆ Do I have the foundation for my own happiness?
- ◆ Do the people in my life contribute to my happiness?
  - ■ Do my family members/relationships support my happiness?
  - ■ Do my coworkers support my happiness?
  - ■ Do my friends support my happiness?
- ◆ If the answer to any of these questions is "no" have I told them what I need them to do or stop doing in order to support my happiness?
  - ■ If not, why not?
  - ■ If you have, why haven't they done it?
- ◆ What kind of additional support do I need to be happy?
  - ■ Are these things, people, time, energy, money, or something else?
  - ■ How can I get them if I do not have them?
  - ■ Can I do this myself or do I need help?
  - ■ Is the help related to time, energy, or money?
- ◆ What next step do I need to take to make my foundation for happiness a success?

When you've answered these questions, think about your answers. After you've honestly and carefully considered your answers, it's time to act on your own happiness, to make the choice to embrace happiness.

Happiness Checklist

This checklist can help you to stay on the path to happiness.

- ◆ Affirm your actions—think of the upside.
- ◆ Be courageous—spend energy where it matters.
- ◆ Adapt a mentality of abundance—there is enough for everyone, including you.

- ◆ Love your life—the sad moments help to make the other moments sweeter
- ◆ Allow and plan—sometimes you need to plan and sometimes you need to just let the moment happen.
- ◆ Find your own wisdom—trust you own voice.
- ◆ Choose happiness—make the choice every day.

Storytelling

Now that you've read the stories of so many working mothers, of all ages, around the globe, in all walks of life and how they have chosen to embrace happiness, it's your turn. Think about the unique person you are, and tell your own story. This is your time to redefine what you want in life and why you want it. Start by accepting who you are and by identifying your strengths.

Telling our stories in life is an important step in our personal mission toward true success as working mothers. It should not matter if we are married or single, employed or self-employed, engaged in life as usual, or entrenched in its challenges. Our purpose in life does not change because our circumstances are not optimal. We simply have to reassess our time frame and how we present ourselves to others who can help us.

A Personal Tale

The power of the story is that it can help open our eyes to what's possible. Jim Loehr, founder of the Human Performance Institute, has helped thousands of competitors in sports and the corporate world capture the best of who they are through the power of story. He details his approach in his book, *Power of Story: Rewrite Your Destiny in Business and in Life* (Free Press, 2007).

To tell your own story, you create a sincere narrative that incorporates order, insight, and love for who you are. It is the true story of your past and your vision for your future. Your story can empower you and help you navigate through troubled times. It is crucial to have an internal voice that helps you communicate your new story to yourself and those around you. Unlike the exercises in previous chapters that focused on specific aspects of your story, this story of you encompasses your overarching mission. The story of you wields great influence by combining the truths of your life, the vocabulary of your life, and the ending that's right for you. Always keep in mind where you would like your story to take you.

Storytelling has long been known to have a profound influence on our performance so be courageous and take the opportunity to create the most powerful story to engage the most powerful person you truly are as a working mother. This is your opportunity to be your own ultimate coach.

How you choose to tell your story reveals much about you. Everyone encounters some twisted threads of failure in the tapestry of their lives. You can either tell your story dwelling on disappointments, or tell the story the way you want others to see you, as the person you would like other people to meet, the most positive version of you. The perspective you take on your story is your choice—as is the option of choosing and committing to happiness.

Authentically Happy

Genevieve Bos was the daughter of a single mother, an artist who worked several jobs to make ends meet. That, Bos says, always left her with the passion to succeed as an adult. As a child, Bos says, she would read the classified ads in the newspaper and say, "I can do that."

"I knew I could effect change doing some of those jobs. . . . I couldn't wait to grow up," says Bos.

And she did. Her successful career has included being publisher of *Business to Business*, Georgia's top business publication, where Bos created numerous sold-out conferences. She spent nearly two decades in international software sales before co-founding *PINK* magazine.

Today Bos is a "virtual" mom for many women she helps in business and in life. Her definition of happiness:

"What you want, when you want it, with whom you want it, and how you want it."

> *Resist peer pressure. Be stubborn; know what you want and go for it. Get rid of the guilt; it does no one any good. Take good care of yourself so you can take care of other people.*
> —Britt van den Berg, director of Global Diversity and Inclusion/
> Talent Recruitment, Philips Corporation

Consider this. When you approach your own story, do you focus on the positive or negative? Do you dwell on your strengths or your weaknesses? You make the choice, and the perspective is up to you. We hope you will embrace the joy, see all that's good in your life, and tell your true story in a positive way.

Loehr suggests you'll probably have to rewrite your story a few times to get it just right. It's worth the effort, though. Having your story on paper truly makes the difference. Keep in mind, too, that your story changes as your life changes.

Your Story

Write down your own story. To help you get started, answer the following questions:

- ◆ What are your strengths?
- ◆ What do you love about yourself?
- ◆ What do you stand for?
- ◆ What do you love most about your kids?
- ◆ What do your kids love most about you?
- ◆ Who is the best you?

Now write a description of who you are. If, for example, you met someone at a get-together and want him or her to know you and like you, what would you say? It must be only the truth.

Thrive—Don't Just Survive

There are days when the demands of being a working mom are so overwhelming that our greatest aspiration is to survive. We just need to get through this project at work or this phase our kids are going through. We just need to hang on long enough for that to be over and then everything will be better.

We challenge you to aim higher than survival. We ask you to make your goal to thrive and flourish. This book has given you the map toward thriving.

Start with the understanding that your happiness is not a luxury; it's a necessity. Understand that the science of happiness shows us that we control our level of happiness through the choices we make. The elements of a happy working mother are:

H—Healthy physically and emotionally

A—Adaptive to changes in circumstances

P—Proud of her family just as they are

P—Proud of her work

Y—Young at heart

You now know that your happiness is the most important element to your children's happiness and that your kids don't suffer as a result of you working, providing that your work makes you happy. When things get tough, reach out for support because no one can do it all alone. And, be authentic. The only person you can be successfully is you and you will be your best when you are happy.

Happiness Tip: Happiness begins when you learn to accept the fact that you are loved and valued for who you are, not what you do.

Congratulations. Reading this book is the first step toward a happier life. Go out and make the decision to be happy every single day.

Mom Corps Survey Analysis

In conjunction with writing *What Happy Working Mothers Know*, we surveyed 773 salaried working women online via our web site survey (www.momcorps.com). Here are some of the results of that survey (http://survey.constantcontact.com/survey/a07e2dl5dhifm29wbaj/results):

Respondent's marital status:

- Married: 87.5%
- Single/divorced: 8.4%
- Single/never married: 3.3%
- Living with partner: <1%

How long have you had this domestic status?

- Less than 5 years: 18.7%
- 5–10 years: 38.5%
- 11–15 years: 19.1%
- 16–20 years: 12.7%
- 21+ years: 10.7%

Which category best describes your annual income?

- Under $50,000: 22.6%
- $50,000–$75,000: 15.2%
- $75,001–$100,000: 18.6%
- $100,001–$125,000: 14.1%
- $125,001–$150,000: 8.1%
- $150,001–$175,000: 6.4%
- $175,001–$200,000: 4.9%

- $200,001–$225,000: 2.8%
- $225,001–$250,000: 2.2%
- $250,001+: 4.7%

Approximately what percentage of your total family income comes from your work?

- Less than 10%: 29.8%
- 10–20%: 7.8%
- 21–30%: 10%
- 31–40%: 9.3%
- 41–50%: 11%
- 51–60%: 7.4%
- 61–70%: 5.4%
- 71–80%: 3.3%
- 81–90%: 2.5%
- 91–100%: 13%

Are you a mother or a guardian?

- Mother: 95.6%
- Guardian: 4.4%

Do you have any children with special needs?

- Yes: 10%
- No: 85.4%

How old were you when you first became a mother?

- Age 16–19: 2.1%
- Age 20–24: 8.4%
- Age 25–29: 25.4%
- Age 30–34: 38.6%
- Age 35–39: 17.7%
- Age 40+: 3%
- No response: 4.4%

If you have a spouse or life partner, what percentage of the child-care responsibilities would you say he/she handles?

- ◆ 0–25%: 39.6%
- ◆ 26–50%: 36.9%
- ◆ 51–75%: 10.7%
- ◆ 76–100%: <1%
- ◆ NA: 7.9%
- ◆ No response: 4.4%

If you are currently working, what arrangements do you have to handle your children's needs when you are at work? Please check all that apply.

- ◆ Not currently in workforce: 22.3%
- ◆ Day care: 22%
- ◆ Live-in nanny: <1%
- ◆ Nanny during work hours: 7.4%
- ◆ After-school programs: 14.1%
- ◆ Kids are old enough to stay home alone: 10.1%
- ◆ Other: 23.4%

How do you think the fact that you're a mother impacts your effectiveness at work?

- ◆ Makes you more effective: 42.4%
- ◆ Makes you less effective: 16.8%
- ◆ Has no impact: 20.8%
- ◆ NA/Not in workforce: 15.4%
- ◆ No response: 4.4%

How do you rate yourself as a mother?

- ◆ Excellent: 28.4%
- ◆ Good: 45.6%
- ◆ Well intentioned, but not always the kind of mother you want to be: 21.2%
- ◆ Not very good: <1%
- ◆ No response: 4.4%

Which of the following categories best describes the industry you work in?

- Advertising: 3%
- Automotive: <1%
- Consulting services: 10%
- Education: 6.5%
- Entertainment: 1.9%
- Financial services: 11.6%
- Government services: 1.9%
- Health care: 3.9%
- Human resources: 8.4%
- Information technology: 6.1%
- Marketing/sales: 12%
- Nonprofit: 3.5%
- Pharmaceuticals: 1.4%
- Public relations: 2.6%
- Technical services: <1%
- Travel: <1%
- Other: 18.3%
- No response: 7.1%

How long have you been working at this or any other job?

- Less than 1 year: 10.9%
- 1–3 years: 16.5%
- 4–6 years: 11.7%
- 7–9 years: 7.5%
- 10–12 years: 13.3%
- 13–15 years: 7.2%
- 16+years: 25.4%
- No response: 7.1%

If you could make one change about your work environment, what would it be?

- Increase your salary: 37.6%
- Increase flexibility in your work schedule: 26.3%

- ◆ Reduce the number of hours you work: 14.7%
- ◆ Reduce the amount of travel required: 1.6%
- ◆ Other: 12.4%
- ◆ No response: 7.1%

Which would you rather have?

- ◆ Unlimited time: 29.1%
- ◆ Unlimited energy: 36.6%
- ◆ Unlimited money: 34.1%
- ◆ Other/no response: <1%

Ten Tips to Your Happiness

◆ Learn to love yourself as much as you love your friends and family. (Chapter 1)
◆ Life happens. What you choose to focus on becomes your experience. Focus on the positive. (Chapter 2)
◆ Learn to forgive yourself and others. (Chapter 3)
◆ Happiness comes from a full, balanced life that includes hard work, time with loved ones and friends, exercise, celebration, and even solitude. Skimp on any of the ingredients, and your recipe for happiness could fall flat. (Chapter 4)
◆ Half the battle in life is choosing something you love to do. The other half is celebrating your successes along the way. (Chapter 5)
◆ When you realize that you're not perfect and allow yourself a few mistakes, you'll go a long way toward being happy. (Chapter 6)
◆ Set the same standards for yourself that you apply to your loved ones; cut yourself the same slack you give others. (Chapter 7)
◆ Knowing when to say "no" and how to do it without feeling guilty increases life satisfaction, and therefore, happiness. (Chapter 7)
◆ You may take a different path from the one you envisioned, but the detours are worth it because you learn more from your failures than from your successes. (Chapter 8)
◆ Happiness begins when you learn to accept the fact that you're loved and valued for who you are, not what you do. (Chapter 9)

Notes

Introduction

1. www.bls.gov/cps/wlf-table7-2008.pdf; www.bls.gov/cps/wlf-intro-2008 .pdf.
2. Dan Baker, Cathy Greenberg, and Collins Hemingway, *What Happy Companies Know* (Prentice Hall, 2006).
3. Community, Families, and Work Program, Brandeis University and Catalyst, http://my.brandeis.edu/news/item?news_item_id=7135.
4. American College of Occupational and Environmental Medicine, Judith A. Ricci, Sc.D.; M.S., Elsbeth Chee, Sc.D.; Amy L. Lorandeau, M.A.; Jan Berger, M.D.; *Journal of Occupational and Environmental Medicine*, 2006; 49 (1): 1-10; www.acoem.org/news.aspx?id=2530.
5. "The Motherhood Study: Fresh Insights on Mothers' Attitudes and Concerns," Martha Farrell Erickson and Enola G. Aird, © 2005 Institute for American Values, reprinted with permission, www.motherhoodproject .org/?cat=23.

Chapter 1: Happiness Is Not a Luxury; It's a Necessity

1. Accenture 2007 Survey.
2. Survey from Working Mother Media; www.digitalforum.accenture.com/ DigitalForum/Global/ViewByTopic/TechnologyCareers/0710_Working _Mothers_Work.htm.
3. Dan Baker, Cathy Greenberg and Collins Hemingway, *What Happy Companies Know* (Prentice Hall, 2006); Rollin McCraty, Ph.D., and Doc Chilre, *The Appreciative Heart: The Psychophysiology of Positive Emotions and Optimal Functioning*, The Institute of HeartMath (2003).
4. Dan Baker, Cathy Greenberg, and Collins Hemingway, *What Happy Companies Know* (Prentice Hall, 2006).
5. "After-School Worries: Tough on Parents, Bad for Business," study from the Women's Studies Research Center at Brandeis University and Catalyst; http://my.brandeis.edu/news/item?news_item_id=7135.
6. American College of Occupational and Environmental Medicine, Judith A. Ricci, Sc.D.; M.S., Elsbeth Chee, Sc.D.; Amy L. Lorandeau, M.A.; Jan

Berger, M.D.; *Journal of Occupational and Environmental Medicine,* 2006; 49 (1): 1-10; www.acoem.org/news.aspx?id=2530.

7. www.iopener.co.uk/happinessatwork.

8. Press release from Hewitt and Associates: www.hewittassociates.com/ Intl/NA/en-CA/AboutHewitt/Newsroom/PressReleaseDetail.aspx? cid=4662

9. www.whatisyourhappiness.com.

Chapter 2: The Science of Happiness

1. Marshall Goldsmith, Cathy Greenberg, Alastair Robertson, and Maya Hu-Chan, from *Global Leadership: The Next Generation,* (Financial Times Prentice Hall, 2003).

2. Press release: www1.umn.edu/umnnews/Feature_Stories/In_search_of _happiness.html.

3. Press release: www1.umn.edu/umnnews/Feature_Stories/In_search_of _happiness.html.

4. Press release: http://us.penguingroup.com/static/html/blogs/what-influences- our-happiness-most-sonja-lyubomirsky.

5. "Biobehavioral Responses to Stress in Females: Tend-and-Befriend, Not Fight-or-Flight," by Shelley E. Taylor, Laura Cousino Klein, Brian P. Lewis, Tara L. Gruenewald, Regan A.R. Gurung, and John A. Updegraff, University of California, Los Angeles; *Psychological Review 2000,* Vol. 107, No. 3, 411-429, ©The American Psychological Association, Inc.; www.apa.org/ journals/rev.html; http://bbh.hhdev.psu.edu/labs/bbhsl/PDF%20files/ taylor%20et%20al.%202000.pdf.

6. Press release: http://medschool.umaryland.edu/innovations.asp.

7. Press release: http://somvweb.som.umaryland.edu/absolutenm/tem plates/?a=630.

8. From PubMed.gov, a service of the U.S. National Library of Medicine and National Institutes of Health; "Psychosocial variables are associated with atherosclerosis risk factors among women with chest pain: the WISE study," Rutledge T., Reis S.E., Olson M., Owens J., Kelsey S.F., Pepine C. J., Reichek N., Rogers W.J., Merz C.N., Sopko G., Cornell C.E., Matthews K.A. (University of Pittsburgh, Pennsylvania); Psychosom Med. 2001 March-April; 63(2):282-8; www.ncbi.nlm.nih.gov/pubmed/11292277.

9. "Emotional Style and Susceptibility to the Common Cold," Sheldon Cohen, Ph.D., William J. Doyle, Ph.D., Ronald B. Turner, M.D., Cuney M. Alper, M.D. and David P. Skoner, M.D.; © 2003 American Psychosomatic Society; from the Department of Psychology (S.C.), Carnegie Mellon University, Pittsburgh; Departments of Otolaryngology (W.J.D., C.M.A.) and Pediatrics (D.P.S.) Children's Hospital of Pittsburgh and the University of Pittsburgh School of Medicine, Pittsburgh, Pennsylvania;

and the Department of Pediatrics (R.B.T.), Medical University of South Carolina, Charleston, South Carolina (now at the University of Virginia Health Sciences Center, Charlottesville, Virginia); Psychosomatic Medicine 65:652-657 (2003); www.psychosomaticmedicine.org/cgi/content/abstract/65/4/652; also citation at http://pmbcii.psy.cmu.edu/cohen/keynotepresentation.pdf.

10. *Monitor on Psychology*, American Psychological Association, "Helping People Flourish Best Boosts Their Mental Health," vol. 36, No. 10 November 2005, 64; www.apa.org/monitor/nov05/flourish.html.

11. "Positive Affect, and the Complex Dynamics of Human Flourishing," Barbara L. Frederickson (University of Michigan), and Marcial F. Losada, (Universidade Católica de Brasília), American Psychologist, ©2005 American Psychological Association, 0003-066X/05, vol. 60, No. 7, 678-686; www.unc.edu/peplab/publications/human_flourishing.pdf.

Chapter 3: How to Put the H.A.P.P.Y. in Happy Working Mother

1. American Dietetic Association, www.eatright.org/cps/rde/xchg/ada/hs.xsl/home_4485_ENU_HTML.htm.

2. More information at www.amenclinics.com/my-brain-health/brain health-club/

3. Web site information: www.eatright.org/cps/rde/xchg/ada/hs.xsl/nutrition_19749_ENU_HTML.htm.

Chapter 4: Guilt—What Is It Good For?

1. Salary.com: www.salary.com/personal/layoutscripts/psnl_articles.asp?tab=psn&cat=cat011&ser=ser032&part=par901.

2. Web site: www.billilee.com/pages/FS1720.tml?page=P1720-16.html.

3. Web site: www.talentplus.com/talent_plus.php?page_id=1013.

4. Web site article: "Men and Women—Differing Drivers in the Development of Senior Executive Talent," Sally Helgesen and Marta Williams; www.sallyhelgesen.com/criticaleye_review.html.

Chapter 5: When Mom's Not Happy, No One Is Happy!

1. Dr. Jody Heymann, founder of the Harvard-based Project on Global Working Families and director of the McGill Institute for Health and Social Policy; "The 2007 Work, Family, and Equity Index: How Does the U.S. Measure Up?" (using updated and expanded data from Heymann's 2004 Harvard study); www.mcgill.ca/files/ihsp/WFEI2007.pdf; www.mcgill.ca/newsroom/news/item/?item_id=23720.

2. 100 Best Companies, *Working Mother Magazine*; www.workingmother.com/?service=vpage/109

Chapter 6: What about the Kids?

1. Press release: www.psy.utexas.edu/psy/announcements/news2005.html; "Maternal employment does not harm infants' development, research shows," press release, March 25, 2005: www.utexas.edu/news/2005/03/25/human_ecology.
2. 1999 study by Elizabeth Harvey, Ph.D., then at the Department of Psychology, University of Connecticut, and now at the University of Massachusetts at Amherst, www.apa.org/journals/releases/dev352445.pdf; American Psychological Association's *Developmental Psychology*, 1999, vol. 35, No. 2 445-459.
3. Compiled by nonprofit Child Trends; www.childtrends.org.
4. From Child Trends: Social Science Research, Washington, D.C.; www.childtrendsdatabank.org/mental.cfm.
5. The Nickelodeon/Talking with Kids National Survey of Parents and Kids, 2000-2001, a survey of parents and their children ages 8 to 15; Talking with Kids is an ongoing campaign of the Kaiser Family Foundation and Children Now; www.talkingwithkids.org/nickelodeon/summary.pdf.
6. "2004 Report Card on The Ethics of American Youth"; www.josephsoninstitute.org/Survey2004.

Chapter 7: When the Going Gets Tough, Get Support

1. 2004 study by Leger Marketing for Wyeth Canada, Courtesy Canadian Mental Health Association; www.cmha.ca/data/1/rec_docs/649_Executive%20Summary%20(ENGLISH)%20Final.pdf.
2. Reprinted courtesy of Renee Peterson Trudeau, © 2007, "The Mother's Guide to Self-Renewal: How to Reclaim, Rejuvenate, and Rebalance Your Life," by Renee Peterson Trudeau; /www.careerstrate gists.net.

Chapter 8: Pulling It All Together

1. Web site, Dr. Joseph J. Luciani: www.self-coaching.net/articles/philosophy_article.php?section=3&ID=87.

Chapter 9: Happily Ever After—Your Story

1. Survey from Working Mother Media: www.digitalforum.accenture.com/DigitalForum/Global/ViewByTopic/TechnologyCareers/0710_Working_Mothers_Work.htm.

Additional Resources

Recommended Reading

Daniel Amen, M.D., *Making a Good Brain Great* (New York: Three Rivers Press, 2005).

Tal Ben-Shahar, Ph.D., *Happier* (New York: McGraw-Hill, 2007).

J. Bort, A. Plfock, and D. Renner, *Mommy Guilt: Learn to Worry Less, Focus on What Matters Most, and Raise Happier Kids* (New York: AMACOM, 2005).

Louann Brizendine, M.D., *The Female Brain* (New York: Broadway Books, 2006).

Lisa Hein, *I'm Doing the Best I Can* (Sirena Press, 2007)

Dr. Wayne W. Dyer, *The Power of Intention* (Carlsbad, CA: Hay House, 2004).

Carol Evans, *This Is How We Do It* (New York: Hudson Street Press, 2006).

Jenifer Fox, *Your Child's Strengths* (New York: Viking Penguin, 2008).

Barbara L. Fredrickson, *Positivity: Groundbreaking Research Reveals How to Embrace the Hidden Strength of Positive Emotions, Overcome Negativity, and Thrive* (New York: Crown, 2009).

Marshall Goldsmith, *Succession: Are You Ready?* (Boston: Harvard Business School Press, 2009).

Marshall Goldsmith, *What Got You Here Won't Get You There: How Successful People Become Even More Successful* (New York: Hyperion, 2007).

Mark Goulston, *Get Out of Your Own Way at Work . . . And Help Others Do the Same: Conquer Self-Defeating Behavior on the Job* (New York: Perigee Trade, 2007).

Betty Holcomb, *Not Guilty! The Good News for Working Mothers* (New York: Touchstone/Simon & Schuster, 1998).

Richard Layard, *Happiness* (New York: Penguin Press, 2005).

Leslie Morgan Steiner, *Mommy Wars: Stay-at-Home and Career Moms Face Off on Their Choices, Their Lives, Their Families* (New York: Random House, 2007).

Deborah Moskovitch, *The Smart Divorce: Proven Strategies and Valuable Advice from 100 Top Divorce Lawyers, Financial Advisers, Counselors, and Other Experts* (Chicago: Chicago Review Press, 2007).

Dee Dee Myers, *Why Women Should Rule the World* (New York: HarperCollins, 2008).

Jeffrey M. Schwartz and Sharon Begley, *The Mind and the Brain* (New York: HarperCollins, 2002).

Marci Shimoff with Carol Kline, *Happy for No Reason* (New York: Free Press, 2008).

Renee Trudeau, *The Mother's Guide to Self-Renewal: How to Reclaim, Rejuvenate, and Rebalance Your Life* (Medina, OH: Balanced Living Press, 2008).

Jamie Woolf, *Mom-in-Chief: How Wisdom from the Workplace Can Save Your Family from Chaos* (Hoboken, NJ: John Wiley & Sons, 2009).

Web Sites

American Heart Association (www.americanheart.org).

Barrett S. Avigdor Working Moms Blog (www.barrettavigdor .com): Co-author, attorney, and coach Barrett S. Avigdor, J.D., blogs for working moms with tips for success at work, at home, and in life.

College of Executive Coaching (www.executivecoachcollege .com): Accredited personal and executive coach training, coaching services, and sophisticated leadership development programs for professionals; free how-to newsletter.

First 30 Days (www.first30days.com): All about positive change with newsletters, expert information, and insights on career, family, fitness, finances, technology, and more.

Barbara L. Fredrickson (http://blogs.psychologytoday.com/ authors/barbara-l-fredrickson-phd): Social psychologist and educator blogs on human flourishing and positivity.

Marshall Goldsmith (www.marshallgoldsmith.com): An executive coaching firm dedicated to developing business leaders.

Cathy L. Greenberg Happiness Blog (www.clgreenberg.com): From author, speaker, consultant, and coach Cathy Greenberg, Ph.D., blogs on happiness, and how companies and individuals can achieve it.

h2c (www.h2cleadership.com): Happy Companies Healthy People is a beacon for happy companies, healthy people, and truly gifted leaders. With its "Happiness = Profit" winning formula for executive development, the company utilizes the science of happiness to achieve outstanding results by transferring coaching knowledge, tools, and techniques through peer networks, and provides enhanced personal awareness and development, greater career success, and increased life satisfaction.

Institute of HeartMath® (www.heartmath.org): Internationally recognized nonprofit research and education organization dedicated to heart-based living—people relying on the intelligence of their hearts in concert with their minds to conduct their lives at home, school, work, and play.

Kyle's Treehouse (www.kylestreehouse.org).

The Marcus Buckingham Company (www.marcusbuckingham .com): From motivational speaker and author Marcus Buckingham.

Mom Corps (www.momcorps.com): Online job information, job postings, staffing solutions, events, services, and more for those who may have opted out of the traditional workforce; designed by a working mom for moms.

Karen Salmansohn (www.notsalmon.com): From the best-selling author, self-help and Bounce Back TV.

Talent Plus (www.talentplus.com): A global human resources consulting firm that for nearly five decades has used scientific studies of success to build high-performing Talent-Based Organizations^{SM} (TBOs).

Renee Trudeau (www.reneetrudeau.com): From the author of *The Mother's Guide to Self-Renewal: How to Reclaim, Rejuvenate, and Rebalance Your Life*, and career and life balance coach and president of Austin, Texas–based Career Strategists; learn all about self-renewal.

True North Leadership Inc. (www.truenorthleadership.com): An executive and organizational development web site that provides innovative management training solutions and executive leadership training programs utilizing emotional intelligence (EI) tools and practices.

U.S. Department of Agriculture (www.nutrition.gov).

w2wlink (www.w2wlink.com): Women, career, networking, and leadership community dedicated to professional women and providing expert knowledge and tools to overcome obstacles and connect with others in the online groups.

What Women Want Study (www.whatwomenwantstudy.com): From Meredith Corp., a leading media and marketing company, and NBC Universal, a 2008 study that asked, "What Do Women Want?"

Wiser Ways to Work® (www.wiserwaystowork.com): Experts in workforce development and management consulting, as well as information resources.

Working Mother Media Survey (www.workingmother.com).

Tools to Explore Your Strengths

American Psychological Association (www.apa.org): Offers a number of tools to help you explore your strengths; check out the APA Help Center.

Center for Creative Leadership (www.ccl.org): Focuses on leadership education and research, and offers expertise in solving the leadership challenges of individuals and organizations.

CPP Inc. (www.cpp.com): Formerly Consulting Psychologists Press, CPP Inc. is a publisher and provider of products, including the Myers-Briggs Type Indicator® (MBTI®) instrument and FIRO-B® instrument (fundamental interpersonal relations orientation-behavior).

Positive Psychology Center/University of Pennsylvania (www.authentichappiness.sas.upenn.edu): From Martin Seligman, director of the University of Pennsylvania Positive Psychology Center and author of *Authentic Happiness* (Simon & Schuster, 2004); includes a number of different questionnaires to help you assess your own well-being in the world around you, including a Children's Strength Survey.

TalentPlus (www.talentplus.com): Experts in the science of talent (see listing under "Web Sites").

About the Authors

Cathy L. Greenberg, Ph.D.

Consultant, Author, Speaker, Coach, Founding Partner, h2c: Happy Companies/Healthy People (www.h2cleadership.com/)

Cathy L. Greenberg is a working mother, and internationally recognized expert on leadership and the science of happiness. As a business consultant, engaging speaker, and a personal and executive coach, she has helped clients ranging from Fortune Global 500 executives to the U.S. military and private individuals maximize their potential using her unique "Happiness=Profit" business formula.

She's won rave reviews from clients as well as from leadership gurus including Warren Bennis, Marshall Goldsmith, Noel Tichy, and Frances Hesselbein, co-founder of the Drucker Foundation and Leader to Leader.

Greenberg, a former managing partner for both Accenture and Computer Sciences Corporation, advises global executives in all industry sectors. To achieve her impressive results, Greenberg conducts leadership and organizational assessments, develops internal coaching networks, and provides direct executive coaching and development based upon proven results.

Her books are mainstays for senior executives and human resource administrators who seek to harness the power of happiness in the workplace. *Global Leadership: Next Generation*, coauthored by Marshall Goldsmith, ranked as the No. 1 leadership book on Amazon.com and Harvard Business Review. Her 2006 book with best-selling coauthor Dan Baker, *What Happy Companies Know: How the New Science of Happiness Can Change Your Company for the Better*, is an international success.

Working with a team of worldwide experts, Greenberg and Bennis completed the most comprehensive work to date with Accenture on developing the Executive of the Future. Their efforts are featured in the Drucker Foundation series Leading Beyond Walls, Coaching for Leadership, and The Future of Leadership with Warren Bennis and a host of experts including Edward Lawler, James Kouzes, Tom Peters, and Mihaly Csikszentmihalyi.

Greenberg has been cited as an authority on leadership and human behavior by all major business and financial news organizations, as well as by popular media outlets such as *O, The Oprah Magazine, Glamour*, and Martha Stewart Living Radio.

Named a "Top 100 Leadership Coach" by *Executive Excellence Magazine* in 2008, she is a highly rated business talk show host on VoiceAmerica Business Network's Leadership Development News.

When not meeting with clients from Sydney to Dubai, Greenberg, mother of one daughter, Elisabeth, divides her time between Philadelphia and Tucson, Arizona. She co-founded and currently serves as the managing partner for h2c: Happy Companies Healthy People.

Barrett S. Avigdor, J.D.
Director Legal Talent Strategy, Accenture, a global management consulting, technology services, and outsourcing company; International Attorney, Career Coach, Speaker, Author

A graduate of the University of Chicago Law School and a former Fulbright Scholar to Brazil, Avigdor has worked at international law firms and, for the past several years, at Accenture, a global business consulting, technology services, and outsourcing company.

In the course of her more than 20-year legal career, Avigdor has built and led international teams of lawyers. She has negotiated large, complex international contracts, has developed and delivered specialized training courses for lawyers all over the world, and mentored dozens of men and women in their legal careers.

Following her passion for coaching, teaching, and learning, Avigdor created the position of Director of Legal Talent Strategy in 2007. In that role, she strives to maximize the productivity, creativity, and engagement of the 400 Accenture legal professionals around the world.

A certified career coach and an advocate for happiness, Avigdor writes and speaks to audiences around the globe on the subject of finding happiness by working to your strengths and aligning your time to your values.

When she's not on the road, she lives in Tucson, Arizona, with her husband, Alain, and their sons Alexander, 17, and Harrison, 14.

Index